VEGETAR

LUNCH BREAK

90 HEALTHY, EASY-TO-MAKE, AND SCHOOL-READY BREAKFAST, SNACK, AND LUNCH RECIPES

EVA ILIANA

CONTENTS

INTRODUCTION: THE VEGETARIAN LIFESTYLE FOR YOUR CHILD

"Let food be thy medicine, and medicine be thy food" (Hippocrates).

These days, health and wellness have taken center stage. Now more than ever, people want to learn more about healthy living and implement these practices in their daily lives. Everywhere you look there are articles, ads, and other resources about healthy foods, vitamin or mineral supplements, and trendy diets. As a parent, trying to keep up with all of these changes can be overwhelming. To make the transition to this different lifestyle easier for you and your kids, it's best to focus on small changes. You should aim for making gradual modifications, instead of bombarding all of these changes in one go to your child's diet.
More and more people have become concerned with their health, and as such, they have started making better food choices. However, nowadays, various food options have become more convenient for the consumer. Everywhere you go, you will see snacks, processed foods, pastries, and more, all of which are extremely appealing to children. Regardless of how convenient and tasty these foods are, they are not good for either you or your child.

So... what should you do?

What can you change to ensure that your child focuses on healthier foods instead of all the junk that is readily available everywhere they go? How do you make nutritious, well-informed choices without sacrificing simplicity, variety, and cost-effectiveness?

If you want to make a change, one of the best things you can do [for yourself] and for your child is to start following a plant-based diet. With proper planning, a plant-based diet such as the vegetarian diet is an excellent choice, especially if you want to make sure that your child will meet all of their nutritional needs. A vegetarian diet involves the elimination of animal flesh (or meat) from the diet. There are different types of vegetarian diets, but this is the most basic one. Some vegetarians, called vegans, don't even eat anything that comes from animals, like eggs or dairy products.

Many people don't think that diets are "right" for children. There is the misconception that they may be lacking or deficient in vitamins, minerals, and nutrients that are essential to a child's growth and development. And that is often true to a point. However, if you plan things right, the vegetarian diet can support your child well. You just need to make sure that whatever you are taking out, is being replaced with a vegetarian-friendly alternative that provides the same nutrients. I myself am a mother, and have chosen this path for my children.

In addition to being an advocate of physical health and wellness, I am a nature-loving person. I encourage other people to adopt healthy lifestyles that support our Earth, which is constantly being over-exploited. Thus, it is important that our food choices reflect not only a healthier lifestyle, but a more environmentally-conscious one as well. Through the years, I have learned, experimented with, and perfected many delicious delicacies using plant-based ingredients.

For the last five years, I have gained a lot of knowledge through rigorous experience and with each day, my passion for this diet grows stronger. Now that I have a profound understanding of the vegetarian diet, I want to share my knowledge to help readers all over the world embrace a greener diet, one which will transform all the aspects of your life in wonderful ways.

While I have successfully helped my two beloved children follow the vegetarian lifestyle, the transition wasn't as easy as I thought [or hoped] it would be. When I started encouraging them to take up the diet, I was still in the process of learning about vegetarianism for children. Because of this, we had a lot of struggles. There even came a time when I wondered if all the challenges were worth it. Of course, deep inside, I knew that what I was doing would benefit my children in different ways. So I kept going. We eventually learned how to compromise and work together to become a family that successfully followed a plant-based diet.

CHAPTER 1

ALL ABOUT THE VEGETARIAN DIET

Those of us who actually follow the vegetarian diet don't think of it as just a 'diet.' It is more of a lifestyle that focuses on plant-based foods and healthier eating habits. As a parent, you must learn as much as you can about the vegetarian diet, especially if you want your child to follow this diet too.

In fact, it's recommended to start following the diet first before you encourage your child to follow suit. That way, you know what the diet involves, how to follow it, and what to expect. Then you can create a plan to help your child.

WHAT IS THE VEGETARIAN DIET?

Although the vegetarian diet has been around for centuries, it has become more popular in recent years. People all over the world have shown interest in this diet, especially now that health and wellness have become more of a priority due to increased research, advancements in medicine and technology, as well as trends. More and more people have turned to plant-based diets to improve their lives.

The most basic definition of vegetarianism is that it involves the elimination of fish, poultry, and meat from your diet. There are various reasons why people make the choice to follow this diet; the major reason is its health benefits. Since this diet mainly focuses on plant-based foods,

it helps improve the quality of your health, promotes weight loss, and even reduces the risk of developing certain chronic diseases. Some people also follow this diet for religious or ethical reasons. For the former, they don't eat meat because their religious beliefs dictate that they shouldn't. For the latter, they might not eat meat because they have a strong belief in animal rights.

Then there are those who have chosen to follow vegetarianism for environmental reasons. They believe that the animal food industry increases the emission of greenhouse gases, contributes greatly to climate change [adversely], and the production of animal food products requires too many natural resources, including energy and water. No matter what your reason is for wanting to follow the vegetarian diet, it would be easier to stick with the lifestyle change by knowing the type of vegetarian diet you will follow. There are many different types of vegetarian diets and their variations lie in their restrictions. The most common types of vegetarian diets include:

- The flexitarian diet, where you only eat fish, poultry, and meat occasionally.

- The Pescatarian diet, where you eliminate poultry and meat while still consuming fish. Also, you allow yourself to consume dairy products (like milk, cheese, butter, and more) and eggs occasionally.

- The Pollotarian diet, where you eliminate fish and meat while still consuming poultry. Also, you allow yourself to consume dairy products (like milk, cheese, butter, and more) and eggs occasionally.

- The lacto-ovo-vegetarian diet, where you eliminate fish, poultry, and meat while still consuming dairy products (like milk, cheese, butter, and more) and eggs.

- The ovo-vegetarian diet, where you eliminate fish, poultry, and meat while still consuming eggs.

- The lacto-vegetarian diet, where you eliminate fish, poultry, and meat while still consuming dairy products (like milk, cheese, butter, and more).

- The vegan diet where you eliminate fish, poultry, and meat along with all other animal-based or animal-derived products like dairy, eggs, and even honey. Some vegans also avoid using products that have been made from animals or involve violations of animal rights such as in cosmetics, clothes, and more.

As a parent, you may follow a more strict vegetarian diet than that of your child, especially if your child has been following a traditional diet since birth. For instance, if you want to go vegan and eliminate all animal foods and products, you may start your child on one of the less restrictive vegetarian diets first. This will help ease your child's transition into vegetarianism without feeling like you are forcing them to follow a diet that is too difficult for them.

BENEFITS OF THE VEGETARIAN DIET

The vegetarian diet focuses on plant-based foods, while some versions of this diet still allow you to consume animal-derived products, like eggs, milk, and cheese. There is no age restriction when it comes to reaping the health benefits of the vegetarian diet. Here are the most common benefits of this diet that you [and your child] can look forward to:

Promotes Weight Loss
When it comes to diets, the most common reason why people follow them is to lose weight. Since the vegetarian diet focuses on foods that are more filling but contain fewer calories, weight loss is a natural effect. As an adult, this is one benefit you want to experience. But for children, losing weight isn't something they have to worry about unless your child is obese. In such a case, your doctor might recommend that you put your child on a diet (like this one) to help them reach a healthy weight. Otherwise, you should balance your child's vegetarian diet well so that they don't end up losing unnecessary weight because of this plant-based diet.

It's Low in Cholesterol
This is one benefit that is good for everyone. Generally, all types of vegetarian diets are associated with lower cholesterol levels. The foods you eat on this diet can help lower your LDL cholesterol level, which is considered 'bad' cholesterol. It also increases your HDL cholesterol levels (referred to as good cholesterol) that your body needs to function to its maximum. For adults, this is important as improving your cholesterol levels can help improve your overall cardiovascular health. By starting your child on a vegetarian diet while they are still young, you will also reduce their risk of developing conditions associated with high cholesterol levels in the future.

Reduces Your Risk of Type-2 Diabetes

The foods you will eat on the vegetarian diet are high in fiber and low on the glycemic index. These foods help stabilize your blood sugar levels, which, in turn, reduce your risk of developing Type 2 diabetes. Even if you are suffering from this condition already, following a vegetarian diet can help you manage the condition better. For children, following this diet can help them prevent getting Type 2 diabetes since they will be eating healthier foods each day. They may experience this benefit even if they follow the "less strict" versions of the diet that allow the consumption of eggs, dairy, and other animal-derived food sources.

Reduces Your Risk of Some Types of Cancer

Amazingly, a vegetarian diet can also reduce your risk of developing [some types] of cancer. In particular, studies have shown that this diet is beneficial in the prevention of rectum, stomach, colon, and breast cancer. While there is a need for more studies and research to link this diet to the prevention of certain cancers, it's still a very important benefit, especially if you have a family history of these devastating diseases.

Promotes Healthy Eating Habits

Since this diet focuses on whole, plant-based foods, it will also teach your child early on to follow healthy eating habits. And if your child can maintain these habits until they grow up, they will have a healthier life as an adult. This is why encouraging your whole family to follow the vegetarian diet is a good move!

POTENTIAL DRAWBACKS OF THE VEGETARIAN DIET

While the vegetarian diet is very healthy and beneficial, it isn't a perfect diet. Just like all other diets out there, this one comes with its own downsides and risks, which is why you need to plan your child's diet carefully before you encourage them to start following it. Here are some of the most significant drawbacks of the diet:

Protein Deficiency

The most common risk of this diet is a deficiency in protein. The reason for this is that meat is the most common protein source available. However, since you will eliminate meat, fish, and poultry from your diet, you need to replace this with enough protein-rich plant-based foods. Otherwise, you might develop a protein deficiency, which has other adverse effects such as edema and even stunted growth in children.

Although plant-based foods are healthy, there are very few options that contain complete proteins. Our body needs nine types of essential amino acids to function optimally. Many animal sources contain all of these amino acids, but this is very rare for plant sources. To avoid this risk, you must focus on high-protein vegetarian foods such as grains, legumes, seeds, nuts, tofu, tempeh, quinoa, and soy. Make sure to include these foods in your child's diet too as they need protein for their growth and development.

Calcium Deficiency

Calcium is another nutrient that might be overlooked when you follow the vegetarian diet, especially when you also eliminate dairy products like cheese and milk. Calcium is an important mineral as it strengthens your teeth and bones while performing other functions around your body too. As it is, most diets are already lacking in calcium. But if you constantly aren't getting enough calcium, it can lead to conditions like osteoporosis or rickets, especially in children. If you want your child to start a vegetarian diet, you may want to continue allowing them to consume high-calcium foods like cheese, yogurt, milk, and other dairy products since they are still growing. As for you, if you are following a stricter version of this diet, you can focus on calcium-rich veggies like turnips, collard greens, and broccoli, for example.

Iron Deficiency

A vegetarian diet may also result in an iron deficiency, which, in turn, may cause appetite loss, extreme fatigue, anemia, and other adverse effects. Iron is especially important for children because if they don't get enough of this mineral, it can cause delayed development and learning problems. For older children, anemia is a big risk, especially during their growth spurts, and when menstrual cycles start in young girls. Fortunately, just like all other nutrient deficiencies, you can avoid these by increasing your consumption of plant-based foods that are rich in iron, like legumes, whole grains, tofu, nuts, leafy green vegetables, and more.

As you can see, the main downside of a vegetarian diet is the risk of developing nutrient deficiencies. You can avoid this by making sure that the diet you follow is well-planned and well-balanced. You may want to speak with your child's doctor before you start them on this diet. That way, you can work together with your child's doctor to create a realistic plan to help with your child's safe transition into this diet.

SUPPLEMENTING ON THE VEGETARIAN DIET

Since nutritional deficiencies are quite common in plant-based diets like a vegetarian diet, you need to learn how to balance your diet properly. As an adult, you can also avoid nutrient deficiencies by taking supplements. Here are some examples of recommended supplements while following the vegetarian diet:

Protein

To ensure that you are getting enough protein, you should include tempeh, tofu, edamame, nut butters, eggs, beans, legumes, amaranth, quinoa, and other types of high-protein foods in your diet. As an adult, you can supplement your vegetarian diet by taking protein pills or protein powders, which are more popular, especially among athletes and people who have active lifestyles. When choosing which protein powder to take, ensure you check the labels. Avoid protein powders that contain added sugars and other artificial ingredients, which don't belong to a healthy diet.

Calcium

To ensure that you are getting enough calcium for the health of your bones, you must include yogurt, cheese, milk, sesame seeds, edamame, almonds, dark green vegetables, tofu, and other types of high-calcium foods in your diet. However, if you have chosen to focus exclusively on plant-based foods, then you can take calcium supplements to get enough of this mineral. There are also some types of multivitamins that contain calcium and other essential nutrients to supplement your diet.

Iron

To ensure that you are getting enough iron, you should include dried fruits (like apricots and prunes), eggs, legumes, beans, fortified cereals, soy, nuts, and other types of high-iron foods in your diet. You can also choose to take iron supplements to avoid an iron deficiency. However, you should not take iron supplements unnecessarily as too much iron can block your body's absorption of other types of minerals, which isn't good for your health. Excessive levels of iron can even cause organ failure or convulsions, which is why you need to have your iron levels checked first before taking iron pills to supplement your diet.

Other Nutrients

While a vegetarian diet is very healthy and beneficial, it may also cause other types of nutrient deficiencies, the most common of which are:

- Zinc
  An essential mineral that boosts your immune system and can be found in eggs, yogurt, cheese, yogurt, and soy products. There are also multivitamins you can take that contain zinc.
- Vitamin B12

It is an essential vitamin that maintains the health of your blood and nerve cells. Vitamin B12 can be found in some types of breakfast cereals, soy-based drinks, and fortified Vegemeat. There are many types of B-vitamin supplements you can take to increase your intake of this vitamin, too.

- Vitamin B2 or Riboflavin
  It is an essential vitamin that plays a significant role in maintaining your body's energy supply. You can get riboflavin from yogurt, cow's milk, fortified milk, soy milk, and mushrooms. If you need this vitamin, you may find B-vitamin supplements that contain vitamin B12, vitamin B2, and other B-vitamins too.

- Alpha-Linolenic Acid or Omega-3
  An essential nutrient that helps with the regulation of genetic function while promoting heart health too. You can get omega-3s from ground flaxseeds, flaxseed oil, walnuts, soybeans, tofu, and canola oil. You can also take omega-3 supplements, which are quite common.

While it's generally safe for adults to take supplements, you should ask your child's doctor first if you're thinking of supplementing your child's diet with protein powders and the like. Of course, it's always best for your child (and yourself) to get all of the nutrients their body needs from the food they eat. That's why it's important to balance your diet and focus on whole, healthy foods.

WHY IS VEGETARIANISM IMPORTANT?

Have you ever wondered why so many people are drawn to the vegetarian lifestyle? Apart from the many health benefits we discussed at the beginning of this chapter, you should know that the vegetarian diet is important for other reasons too. These include:

It's Environmentally-Friendly
The animal food industry is really taking a toll on our planet. If more people follow the vegetarian diet, this can help reduce the environmental effects of the industry that produces food from animals. When you switch to the vegetarian diet, you can already reduce your environmental footprint more significantly than if you would start using a hybrid car. Plus, plant-based foods are much more sustainable than food derived It Maintains the Balance of the Ecosystem

It Maintains the Balance of the Ecosystem

Apart from being more eco-friendly, vegetarian diets also help bring balance to the ecosystem. If there is a reduction in meat consumption all over the world, we can allow depleted habitats to replenish themselves. For instance, since fish is a very popular food, populations of fish around the globe have been overfished to the point where there are very little left. The same thing goes for livestock and other kinds of animals, too. This diet might seem simple, but if more people start following it, we can contribute to the overall improvement of the health of our planet.

It's Morally Ethical

Finally, another common reason why people switch to the vegetarian diet is that it's more ethical. If you ever learn how all kinds of animals are being treated in food factories and food farms, you will be horrified. Animals are being bred, raised, and slaughtered using inhumane practices in deplorable conditions to provide enough food for people all over the world. When people learn about this industry and what is involved in the production of animal-based and animal-derived food, they asre more likely to make the choice to shift to more ethical options. This is also one of the more common reasons why people choose to stop using clothing, cosmetics, and other products that involve animal abuse as well.

CONTROVERSIES SURROUNDING THE VEGETARIAN DIET

The vegetarian diet is becoming more popular by the day, but this doesn't mean that everyone perceives it in a positive way. Despite the wonderful benefits this diet has to offer, it still remains quite controversial. This is mainly because those who don't follow the diet feel like vegetarians are always trying to get everyone else to make the same choices.

Of course, this isn't true at all.

One of the reasons why vegetarianism is widespread is that vegetarian beliefs are at common loggerheads with religious practices all over the world. For instance, those who practice Jainism follow the vegetarian diet as it is mandatory for them. For those who practice Buddhism and Hinduism, some of them follow this diet too as it is advocated by religious authorities and influential scriptures. And although the mainstream authorities of Islam, Judaism, and Christianity don't enforce previous traditional dietary rules and restrictions, some of their believers follow them anyway as part of their beliefs.

These are just some examples of how vegetarianism is strongly associated with religious beliefs. For this reason, a lot of people believe that people should only follow it as an expression of their faith. The good news is, this belief is slowly fading away as more and more people are getting interested in vegetarianism and other plant-based diets.

Another controversial aspect of the vegetarian diet is whether people who follow this diet are getting adequate nutrition. Many people believe that plant-based foods aren't enough to provide human beings with the nutrients we need to survive and thrive. After all, our hunter-gatherer ancestors survived mainly on meat and only foraged for plants, nuts, and seeds when there were no animals to hunt. But that is all in the past. These days, we have access to different types of plants and plant-based food items to make our diets satisfying and nutritious.

Thanks to researchers and food experts, we are also more knowledgeable in terms of what we should eat in order to get all of the recommended nutrients we need every day. Still, this remains to be a common issue that makes people feel reluctant to try this diet. Of course, when people truly learn what the vegetarian diet is all about, they discover that it's a healthy, sustainable, easy-to-follow diet that offers a lot of benefits. Those who follow the vegetarian diet already know this. If more people try to learn about this diet, it won't be as controversial or seemingly unfamiliar or daunting as it is now.

CHAPTER 2

IS GREEN THE WAY TO GO?

If you ask a vegetarian this question, their answer will be a most definite yes.

But if you're still on the fence for yourself or your child, then you need to learn more. In fact, it's important for you to learn everything you can about this diet before you make a decision so that you're not blindly following what someone else tells you to do. You should be able to make a well-researched and well-informed decision that is right for you. Changing your diet to one that eliminates entire food groups (meat, fish, and poultry) requires a lot of planning – even more so if you want your child to follow the diet too. So let's answer some of the most important questions and discuss the most important concerns about the vegetarian diet in this chapter.

WHY SHOULD YOU CONSIDER THE VEGETARIAN DIET FOR YOUR CHILD?

As an adult, following the vegetarian diet isn't that challenging unless you are a hardcore carnivore and you don't usually eat plant-based foods. But when it comes to your child, there are more concerns or considerations to think about before you encourage them to follow this diet. Often, people who were already vegetarians when they became parents would choose to let their children follow the same lifestyle, too.

But if you have just transitioned into a vegetarian diet yourself and you're considering the same for your child, it's important to plan this diet carefully. If a child chooses to become a vegetarian because they learned about it in school, they discovered the truth behind the animal food industry and they don't want to eat another animal, or for any other reason, helping your child transition into this diet would be much easier.

But if it is your choice to encourage your child to follow this diet, then you may have to explain the reasons why you want this lifestyle for them. Also, you would have to be more patient and encouraging throughout the process to make it easier for both of you.

But before you begin, have you ever thought about why you should consider a vegetarian diet for your child?

If you are still wondering why this diet is a great choice for children, here

are some reasons for you:

- Vegetarian recipes use simple ingredients that are easy to find, prepare, cook, and serve. This means that even if you're a beginner in the kitchen, you will be able to prepare healthy and tasty dishes for your child.
- Since vegetarian meals are much easier and faster to prepare, you will save a lot of time each day. This, in turn, will allow you to do other things around the house.
- You won't have to worry about whether your child is eating healthy food or not. If you plan your child's vegetarian diet carefully, then you will always feel confident that they are being nourished by delicious and nutritious food each day.
- Of course, if you are following the same diet as your child, you can also make sure that you are maintaining your own health and well-being.
- Fruits and vegetables are much cheaper than animal-based products. And if you learn how to store vegetarian ingredients well, you can preserve them longer. This means that you can save a lot of money, too.
- Many vegetarian recipes are easy to make. You can involve your child in the food-making process, which can be a fun activity for them. This would also be an excellent opportunity to teach your child about healthy foods and why you want your child to follow the vegetarian diet.

Following a vegetarian diet ensures that your whole family's food supply is rich in nutritional value. With all of these reasons, it's clear that a vegetarian diet is definitely a healthy lifestyle to choose for people of all ages.

IS VEGETARIANISM COOL FOR SCHOOL?

If you are thinking about helping your child transition into a vegetarian diet, you should also consider the other aspects of their life. While the transition may be easy at home, especially if all the other members of your family go vegetarian, the situation at school might be very different. However, changing your child's diet to a plant-based one definitely has long-term advantages:

- Following a healthy, plant-based diet will keep your child's body slim and at a healthy weight, which is a definite confidence booster. This is especially important as your child grows and becomes more aware of their appearance.

- Plant-based foods will keep your child energized throughout the day, which is very important, especially while they are at school.

- Going vegetarian might make your child more popular as plant-based diets have become very trendy these days.

- You and your child will get opportunities to attend social events and club activities that advocate the vegetarian diet.

- Your child will become knowledgeable in eating healthy foods at a young age. And if you involve your child in preparing their own food, this might even awaken their interest in cooking their own vegetarian dishes.

Of course, depending on your child's school environment, there might still be issues like rejection, embarrassment, and/or peer pressure. This is especially true if there are very few vegetarians in your child's school. In such a case, you may want to communicate with your child's teacher about the journey your child is about to take.

To help your child adjust mentally and emotionally to the diet even if all the other kids at school are eating different foods, you must provide a strong support system. If you can spread this awareness to your whole family, your child's teacher, and even their closest friends, your child's transition will become a positive learning experience for them.

IS IT EASY TO LEARN VEGETARIAN DISHES?

Yes, it is!

From simple breakfast options like chia pudding to snacks that take no time at all like apple crackers, vegetarian recipes are a breeze to learn. And the best part is, the recipes you make for your child can be enjoyed by the whole family, too. In the last chapters of this book, you will learn a bunch of new recipes with varying levels of difficulty. There are recipes that require very few ingredients and very little time to make, while there are also recipes that are more intricate and time-consuming, but very well worth it.

Either way, any competent cook will be able to follow the recipes in this book to create amazingly delicious and healthy dishes for children. Another great thing about vegetarian recipes is that you can mix and match the ingredients. As you will discover later, there are recipes that will teach you the basic methods for cooking certain dishes, but you have the freedom to choose which plant-based ingredients to use. A lot of ingredients are interchangeable. There are even some recipes that are so simple that you can teach them to your child so that they can prepare their own snacks at home whenever they're hungry. So if you plan to go vegetarian, cooking your meals isn't something you have to worry about!

IS VEGETARIAN FOOD CONVENIENT?

Yes, it is.

While choosing, buying, preparing, and storing animal-based foods can be quite challenging, this isn't something you have to deal with when you're on a vegetarian diet. Apart from being super affordable, you can buy different kinds of fruits and vegetables from any supermarket or food store. Even though some of these fresh produce are only available in certain seasons, you can buy them in bulk and then store them in your freezer for a long period. That way, you can serve your child's favorite fruits and veggies even when they aren't in season!

To successfully store your fruits and veggies, you need to know how to store them properly. For instance, you may have to blanch some types of veggies before freezing them. In the case of fruits, there are some fruits that you need to ripen first before you place them in the freezer. Knowing these storage tips will make using vegetarian ingredients even more convenient for you. Here are the basic storage tips for you to remember:

Storing Fruits

Before you store fruits, you should first decide how you will use them. Often, it is better to prepare the fruits before storing them so when it's time to use them in your dishes, all you have to do is thaw the fruits. For instance, if you buy strawberries and you plan to use them in a pie, core the strawberries and slice them before freezing. Or if you buy different kinds of fruits to make quick smoothies, cut them into chunks before freezing. You can look at the recipes you plan to make to give you an idea of how to prep the fruits before storing them. No matter how you plan to use fruits, you need to do the following:

- Rinse the fruits using hot water from the tap then use a dish towel to dry the fruits thoroughly. For soft fruits, it's best to air-dry them so they don't end up getting squished or bruised.
- Prepare the fruits according to how you plan to use them.
- Use parchment paper to line a baking sheet, then place the prepared fruits on top in a single layer. Place the baking sheet in the freezer until the fruits have become solid.
- Transfer the fruits to a freezer bag, reusable silicone bag, or an airtight container (don't mix them!) and then place them in the freezer. You can usually freeze fruits for up to three months.

Knowing how to store these will help save you a lot of time and money. Here are some tips:

- Allow avocados to ripen first before storing them in the refrigerator.
- Store citrus fruits in a mesh bag or in your refrigerator's crisper drawer to make them last longer.
- Store berries, grapes, and cherries in an airtight container. Store berries while dry and only wash them right before you use or serve them.
- Store tomatoes in a cool, dry place instead of the refrigerator

Storing Vegetables

When it comes to storing vegetables, it's best to store those which you need to cook first before eating—not the ones you can eat raw like lettuce, cabbage, and cucumbers. As with fruits, there are certain steps to follow when storing veggies as well:

- Rinse the veggies thoroughly first, then either air-dry them or use a paper towel to dry the veggies well.
- Prepare the vegetables according to how you will need them. For this step, refer to the recipes you plan to follow.
- For most vegetables, it's best to blanch them first so that they keep their color without losing their texture or nutrient content.
- Use parchment paper to line a baking sheet, then place the prepared veggies on top in a single layer. Place the baking sheet in the freezer until the veggies have become solid.
- Transfer the vegetables in a freezer bag or an airtight container then place it in the freezer. You can usually freeze vegetables for up to three months.

As with fruits, there are certain vegetables used in common dishes that require special care. You should know how to store these, too. Here are some tips:

- When storing cauliflower and broccoli, keep them away from other vegetables in the refrigerator.
- Store onions and garlic in a cool, dry, and dark space away from other food items.
- Cucumbers, peppers, and eggplants are best stored at room temperature, but you can also keep them in your refrigerator for up to three days.
- Store celery, beets, radishes, carrots, green beans, green leafy vegetables, and corn in the refrigerator. For corn, don't remove the husks yet.
- Store mushrooms in an airtight container. Store mushrooms while dry and only wash them right before you use them.

The more you experiment with different kinds of fruits and vegetables, the more you will learn how to store them properly. Soon, you will become a true vegetarian master chef!

THINGS TO CONSIDER BEFORE GOING VEGETARIAN

As you think of the steps to help your child start a vegetarian diet, there are many things to consider. Think about how your child will adjust to the diet at home, in school, and other places too. You need to make small changes to your child's diet over time rather than forcing them to change what they eat overnight. Starting a new diet means that you will have to change your daily routine, too. When you have made the decision to go vegetarian with your child, here are some considerations to keep in mind:

- Whenever you eat out, you must first check with the restaurant if they offer vegetarian options. Fortunately, this is much easier to do today as you can check restaurant menus online.
- You need to give your pantry, kitchen, and refrigerator a makeover. This means getting rid of non-plant-based ingredients and only buying foods that belong to your diet from here on out.
- Whenever it's time for you to shop at supermarkets, bring a list of things you need to buy. That way, you don't end up buying items on impulse or even buying foods that don't belong to your diet just because you have always been buying them.
- It's best to inform the people closest to you like your relatives,

friends, and important people at your child's school. That way, they can help with the transition too.

It would also be useful if you learn how to substitute food products to supplement the lack of certain nutrients from the foods you will eliminate from your diet. Also, learn how to substitute ingredients in non-vegetarian recipes so that you can continue to cook your favorite dishes even if you are following a new diet.

When you start following a vegetarian diet, you may notice a number of changes happening to your body. These include:

- A more positive mood each day.
- Changes in your smell sensitivity and taste preference.
- A feeling of being refreshed.
- An improvement in your complexion.
- A slight effect on your fatigue levels, especially at the beginning of your transition.
- Faster body recovery.
- A drastic improvement in your sleep cycle.
- Hunger tendencies decrease while water consumption increases.
- Changes in hormonal levels.

It's important to observe your child very carefully as you help them start the diet, so that you can monitor them for any changes (positive or negative). This is also why it's important to make small, consistent changes to give your child's body time to adjust to the new foods, and not shock their system.

TIPS FOR VEGETARIAN BEGINNERS

The vegetarian diet is truly a healthy option for the whole family. Still, you need to make adjustments to your daily routine and the other aspects of your life to make it easier to transition into the diet and continue following it long-term. The beginning is always the hardest part. But with the right set of tips and strategies, you can make this journey a positive one. Here are some important tips to help you out:

- Make a plan for your new diet. Come up with a list of goals and a list of steps for how to achieve those goals. Be as specific as possible when writing them down to make it easier for you to follow your plan.
- Always include dark-colored vegetables in your meals as these are the most nutrient-dense ones. Have these veggies at least three times each week.
- Eat the rainbow! This is a very common piece of advice that is applicable no matter what diet you're following. To make your diet more interesting, make sure to eat fruits and veggies of different colors. You can have some raw fruits and veggies as snacks—just make sure to rinse them well first. If you feel hungry or you're craving something, prepare a bowl of salad (fruit salad if you want something sweet, veggie salad if you want something savory). These are some examples of how you can start eating more fruits and veggies. This is a great tip for children too.
- Make sure that you are always well-hydrated. If you can, try to aim for eight liters of water a day, or even more if you can!
- Reduce your intake of refined and processed sugar. This is something to aim for once your child is used to the vegetarian diet already.
- Consult with your doctor to ask if you need to take supplements for iron, protein, calcium, vitamin B12, and other nutrients. You may even opt for multivitamins, which contain more than one type of nutrient.

Simple as these tips are, they really work! And always remember to take things slow so that you don't feel too stressed while starting your new diet.

CHAPTER 3

ENCOURAGING YOUR FAMILY TO GO VEGETARIAN TOO

The path to righteousness (also known as the vegetarian diet) can be very challenging unless you can get your whole family on board. While you don't have to force them to follow the same diet as you, encouraging your family by showing them how easy it is to follow the diet and how beneficial it can be for them and the planet will increase your chances of convincing them to go green. Even as a parent, you should focus on encouraging your child to follow this diet instead of imposing it upon them. In this chapter, we will discuss your role as a parent and how you can encourage your child [and the rest of your family] to start following this amazing plant-based diet.

YOUR ROLE AS A PARENT

A well-planned vegetarian diet is healthy, nutritious, and highly beneficial. Now that you are thinking about involving your child in your vegetarian journey too, you should know exactly what role you play as a parent.

As with almost everything in family life, it has to start from the top. Usually, children follow their parents' footsteps, especially while they are still young. You can use this as an opportunity to encourage your child to follow the plant-based diet with you. If you plan to do this, remember that you play a very important role in the process. It's up to you to start transitioning your daily meals intermittently. For instance, once a day, you can serve a vegetarian meal, either for breakfast, lunch, or dinner. Do this everyday or every other day to get your family used to vegetarian dishes more often.

If your child doesn't want to eat the [vegetarian] dish you have prepared, don't scold or reprimand them. Since you are still in the process of introducing the vegetarian diet, be patient. If possible, encourage the other adults in your household to try the dishes so that your child will also feel compelled to give them a try. Keep the whole atmosphere positive so you don't end up making vegetarianism "the enemy" in your child's eyes.

You need to accept the fact that people adjust differently to dietary changes. Some children are more willing to try new foods while others would need weeks or even months of encouragement just to try one dish. This is okay. Just keep encouraging your child and offering them vegetarian advice until they finally agree to eat a vegetarian dish you have prepared. As you are doing this, you can also give these other tips a try:

- Create a list of vegetarian meals to prepare starting with the first week when you decide to follow this diet.
- Plan "restaurant days" where you choose a place that serves vegetarian-friendly food. Once there, order different kinds of plant-based dishes. This tip requires some research as you should find restaurants in your locale that serve the food you're looking for. Do this beforehand so that you are not surprised, disappointed, or caught off-guard.
- Bring your child to local fruit stores or vegetable plantations to make them feel more interested in plant-based foods. This activity will increase their awareness of how healthy and wonderful a vegetarian diet can be.
- Join vegetarian communities and online forums to learn more about how to transition into the diet and how to encourage your family to join you, while exchanging valuable ideas and experiences with others. It is helpful to give and receive support from like-minded community, because you can help each other.

As you do all of these things, you should always be mindful of the nutrients that your child is getting each day. As a parent, you should make sure that all the meals and snacks your child eats throughout the day provide them with all the vitamins and minerals they need to grow healthy and strong.

WHAT ROLE DOES YOUR CHILD PLAY?

While there is much for you to do throughout your vegetarian diet journey with your family, your child has a couple of roles to play, too. When it comes to this kind of lifestyle change, you need to communicate openly with your child, especially if they are old enough to understand. After talking to your child about the vegetarian diet, you can ask them to contribute to the success of your journey by:

- Speaking to you politely and openly about what they think about the transition. If they have any concerns or questions, they can talk to you. This is especially true for older children.
- Encourage them to give the vegetarian diet a chance. Instead of complaining about everything, motivate your child to try new things

and adjust to the changes in their diet happily.

- Ask them to help you out in the kitchen so that they gain hands-on experience in terms of preparing healthy, plant-based dishes. In the process, they can also suggest recipes that you can make in the kitchen together.
- Talk to their friends, teachers, and the other members of your family about the vegetarian diet. This will give them valuable insights about the diet while gaining some good advice on how they can deal with all of the changes and help your child to the best of their ability.

TRANSITIONING INTO VEGETARIANISM AS A FAMILY

Now that you know your roles as a parent and the roles of your child in your vegetarian diet journey, it's time to start your transition as a family. Apart from all of the tips we have already discussed, there are certain family activities you can do to make the transition a more enjoyable one. These include:

Grocery Shopping

If you will be planning your meals, it would be better to set aside a specific day to shop for all of the ingredients you need to make those meals. Your trip to the grocery store would also involve stocking up on basic kitchen supplies that are running low. Whenever you go to the supermarket, it's best to bring a list with you so you can avoid over buying or purchasing things you don't need. You can involve your children in this activity by letting them create different lists. For instance, for older children, you can give them a list of all the fruits or vegetables you need. Give your child the list and ask them to find all of the items on it. As a reward, you can allow your child to choose one plant-based snack item from the shelves. This activity is fun and it will also teach your child to identify the ingredients they will use while cooking with you.

Experimenting With Food

Involving your child in preparing and cooking their meals is an amazing way to encourage them to eat more plant-based foods. It also prepares them to be more independent and inclined to cook this way even when you're not around. When you have taught your child some basic kitchen skills, you can start experimenting with them. Come up with your own family dishes to make cooking more fun!

Growing Your Own Food

This is another enjoyable and educational activity you can do at home. If you have a big garden, you can plant some fruits and veggies outside. If you don't have space outside, you can always start a micro garden inside your home, or on a small balcony if you live in an apartment. Either way, the whole process of planting seeds, watching them grow, and harvesting the fruits, veggies, and herbs will be an amazing experience for your child that will make them feel more willing to follow the vegetarian diet. This will also ensure you always have fresh ingredients at hand, free from harmful chemicals and pesticides. Plus, it will give you and your children a better appreciation for the earth.

The great thing about children is that they respond very quickly to positive experiences. The more creative and fun you are with the activities you come up with, the easier it will be for your child to start following this diet with you.

POTENTIAL DANGER SIGNS TO LOOK OUT FOR

Whenever you start a new diet, part of the process is to observe how your body is reacting to it. As healthy as the vegetarian diet is, there are still some potential danger signs to look out for that may indicate that something is wrong. After speaking with your child's doctor about shifting them to a vegetarian diet, you should also be on the lookout for any unusual signs in case they occur.

Stomach Bloating

While many fruits, vegetables, and grains are healthy and satisfying, they can also cause gas, cramping, and bloating, especially if your child consumes too many of these foods in a single meal. Encourage your child to drink more water, which will make it easier for their bodies to digest their food to prevent bloating and similar issues.

Excessive Weight Gain

One of the common benefits of the vegetarian diet is weight loss. So if your child starts gaining weight excessively, there might be something wrong with how they are following the diet. In such a case, you should check your child's portion sizes even though they are mainly eating plant-based foods. Or, it could indicate another problem entirely that they might need to get checked out by a doctor. Either way, just be aware of any major physical changes your child is going through, that way you can keep them as safe and healthy as you possibly can.

Appetite Loss

There are some types of fruits and veggies that cause appetite loss because your child will feel satisfied for longer periods. This is okay. But if appetite loss happens because your child only eats processed plant-based foods instead of healthy, whole options, then you need to encourage them to focus on healthier fare.

Persistent Hunger

If your child is always hungry even though you serve their meals and snacks on time, this may be an indication that your child isn't getting enough protein. High-protein foods are more filling and they take a longer time to digest. You may want to include high-protein foods in your child's meals so they don't feel hungry all the time.

Constant Fatigue or Lethargy

These things may happen if your child eats too many grains and bread without getting enough healthy fats and lean proteins. Ideally, each of your child's meals should contain a healthy fat source (like avocados) and a protein source (like tofu or eggs). Balancing your child's meals will help increase their energy levels instead of making them feel tired and sluggish.

It's important to keep observing your child, especially at the beginning of their vegetarian diet. If you observe any of these signs or symptoms, you should make some changes to their diet. This will ensure that you are accommodating your child's unique body requirements to make the diet more suitable for them.

CHAPTER 4

STARTING YOUR CHILD'S DAY WITH THE RIGHT KIND OF FOOD

The path to righteousness (also known as the vegetarian diet) can be very challenging unless you can get your whole family on board. While you don't have to force them to follow the same diet as you, encouraging your family by showing them how easy it is to follow the diet and how beneficial it can be for them and the planet will increase your chances of convincing them to go green. Even as a parent, you should focus on encouraging your child to follow this diet instead of imposing it upon them. In this chapter, we will discuss your role as a parent and how you can encourage your child [and the rest of your family] to start following this amazing plant-based diet.

THE IMPORTANCE OF A HEALTHY BREAKFAST

Do you know that breakfast is the meal that literally "breaks a fast?"

As your child sleeps throughout the night, they won't be eating anything. When they wake up, they need to nourish their body with a healthy meal for their body to start working effectively once again. Breakfast is the meal that kick-starts your child's whole day, offering the following benefits:

- It replenishes the body's essential components, which it needs to rejuvenate itself.
- It promotes the health of the brain while boosting brainpower too.
- It increases energy levels by supplying fat, carbohydrates, protein, and other essential nutrients needed for various bodily functions.
- It provides a wide range of minerals and vitamins (depending on the dish) to keep the body strong and healthy.
- It starts regulating the appetite, which aids in the maintenance of healthy body weight. By eating a healthy, filling breakfast, your child won't end up making poor food choices later in the day.
- It helps reduce the risk of illnesses.

With all of these important benefits of this morning meal, you should make sure that your child never misses breakfast, especially on school days. And if you always serve a nutritious breakfast, your child will surely enjoy these benefits each day.

FOODS YOU SHOULD AVOID WHEN PREPARING BREAKFAST

Since the responsibility of preparing a healthy breakfast for your child lies with you, it's important to know the healthiest options to serve them. While it's much easier to go with convenient, ready-made foods, these options won't contribute to the overall health and well-being of your child. What's more, there are certain foods that can ruin your child's digestive process throughout the day if these are the first things they eat after their six to eight-hour fast. Some foods to avoid when preparing breakfast include packet oatmeal, cereals that are high in sugar (especially when you serve this every morning), and fast food (burgers, chicken nuggets, sausage-egg biscuits, hash browns, and anything else that comes from a fast-food joint). In terms of beverages, carbonated drinks are a huge no-no. As for you and any other adults in your family, you should avoid drinking instant coffee on an empty stomach.

FOCUS ON THESE INGREDIENTS WHEN MAKING YOUR CHILD'S MEALS

While there are foods you should avoid when preparing breakfast for your child, there are also foods which are recommended. When preparing your child's food or cooking vegetarian dishes for them, you should always try to include the following foods:
- Avocados, either served on their own or as part of a dish.
- Berries like strawberries, blueberries, or blackberries.
- Eggs with both the yolks and the egg whites.
- Greek yogurt or any natural, plain yogurt products.
- Seeds, such as chia seeds and flaxseeds.
- Whole-grains like farro, quinoa, millet, and buckwheat.

You can even include fresh fruits and veggies into your child's breakfast by mixing them together in a quick and nutritious smoothie. Just make sure you are combining the fruit with some dry oatmeal or a protein (like peanut butter) to make it filling and cut down on the amount of sugar. These are just some examples of essential foods to include in your child's breakfasts each day. Later, you will discover more ingredients as you go through the healthy breakfast recipes in this chapter.

WHY BREAKFAST SHOULDN'T BE SKIPPED

No matter how busy you are, you should try to enjoy a nutritious and tasty breakfast with your child everyday. They don't even have to be complex dishes, as long as they contain nutrient-dense ingredients. This is especially true for your child. Although you may skip breakfast once in a while without experiencing any adverse effects, making a habit out of skipping this important meal may cause certain adverse effects:

- Your body's metabolism slows down since it feels like it needs to conserve energy (because you didn't eat anything since you woke up).
- Increased stress levels, especially when you feel hungry, and you know that you have to wait until lunch to satisfy your hunger.
- Adverse effects on your cognitive functioning, especially when you need to do important things at work.
- Headaches and migraines, which are caused by low levels of blood sugar.
- An increased risk of developing illnesses like Type 2 diabetes and even cancer.
- Weight gain, especially if you end up bingeing on your next meal.

If you go back to the benefits of breakfast, you will see how important it is. Now that you know what may happen if you keep skipping breakfast, it's time to make a change. Once you skip your first meal of the day, you will lose all the potential benefits that come with it, too. With this realization, it's time to learn some recipes you can make in your kitchen now...

PLANT-BASED BREAKFAST RECIPES TO START THE DAY

NOW THAT YOU KNOW HOW IMPORTANT BREAKFAST IS, YOU CAN START COOKING SOME TASTY AND HEALTHY DISHES FOR YOUR CHILD. THE BEST PART ABOUT THESE RECIPES IS THAT THEY'RE SUPER EASY! EVEN THE REST OF YOUR FAMILY CAN ENJOY THESE BREAKFAST DISHES, TOO.

HEALTHY OVERNIGHT OATS

This recipe is the perfect to-go breakfast that's a breeze to prepare. It's healthy, tasty, and perfect for your whole family.

TIME: 20 minutes
(chilling time not included)

 SERVING SIZE: 2 servings

PREP TIME: 10 minutes

COOK TIME: no cooking time

INGREDIENTS:

- ¼ tsp cinnamon (ground)
- 2 tsp honey
- 2 tbsp coconut flakes
  (unsweetened, toasted)

- ½ cup of blueberries
- ½ cup of strawberries (sliced)
- ⅔ cup of old-fashioned rolled oats
- 1⅓ cups of kefir (plain, low-fat)

DIRECTIONS:

1. In a bowl, add the kefir, rolled oats, honey, and cinnamon then mix well.

2. Cover the bowl and place it in the refrigerator.

3. The next morning, scoop the mixture into serving bowls.

4. Top each bowl with coconut flakes, blueberries, and strawberries, then serve.

PLANT-BASED BREAKFAST CASSEROLE

This tasty casserole is perfect for breakfast for your whole family. It contains healthy ingredients that are combined into a winning dish.

 TIME: 50 minutes

SERVING SIZE: 8 servings

PREP TIME: 10 minutes

COOK TIME: 40 minutes

INGREDIENTS:

- ½ tsp fine salt
- 1 tbsp extra-virgin olive oil
- 3 tbsp full-fat heavy cream
- ¾ cup of green onion (thinly sliced)
- 1 cup of feta cheese (crumbled)

- 5 cups of spinach (roughly chopped)
- 2 red bell peppers (chopped)
- 12 eggs
- Black pepper
- Butter (for greasing the baking pan)

DIRECTIONS:

1. Preheat your oven to 350°F and use some butter to grease a baking pan.

2. In a skillet, add the olive oil over medium heat.

3. Add the green onion and bell pepper, then cook for about 8 to 10 minutes.

4. Add the chopped spinach and continue cooking for about 2 minutes until wilted.

5. Take the skillet off the heat and set aside.

6. In a bowl, add the eggs, heavy cream, salt, and pepper and whisk until just blended.

7. Add half of the cheese and continue mixing to combine.

8. Add the veggie mixture into the bowl then continue mixing to combine.

9. Pour the casserole mixture into the baking pan and top with the rest of the cheese.

10. Place the baking pan in the oven and cook the casserole for about 25 to 35 minutes. Use a fork to check if the inside of the casserole is properly cooked. Stick the fork into the casserole and if it comes out clean, it's done!

11. Take the baking pan out of the oven and allow the casserole to cool down before you slice and serve

SWEET POTATO BREAKFAST HASH

Making a hash for your child will make them more interested in eating veggies for breakfast. This dish is crispy, savory, and super healthy.

TIME: 30 minutes

SERVING SIZE: 1 serving

PREP TIME: 15 minutes

COOK TIME: 15 minutes

INGREDIENTS:

- ⅛ tsp cumin (ground)
- ⅛ tsp kosher salt
- ¼ tsp chili powder
- 1½ tsp olive oil (divided)
- 2 tsp water
- 1 tbsp cilantro (fresh, chopped)

- 2 tbsp avocado sauce
- ¼ cup of black beans (unsalted, canned, rinsed, drained)
- ⅔ cup of red bell pepper (chopped)
- ¾ cup of sweet potato (peeled, diced)
- 1 large egg

DIRECTIONS:

1. In a microwave-safe dish, add the sweet potatoes and water then use food-grade plastic wrap to cover the dish.

2. 2Place the dish in the microwave on high for about 4 minutes.

3. Transfer the potatoes to a plate lined with a paper towel and allow to cool down for about 5 minutes.

4. In a skillet, add 1 teaspoon of olive oil over medium-high heat.

5. Add the bell pepper, chili powder, sweet potatoes, cumin, and salt,

then cook for about 6 to 8 minutes until the sweet potatoes are crisp.

6. Add the black beans and continue cooking for about 1 to 2 minutes.

7. Transfer the mixture to a plate.

8. Turn the heat down to medium and add the remaining olive oil.

9. Crack the egg into the pan and cook for about 3 to 4 minutes while stirring.

10. Top the sweet potato hash with the scrambled egg, cilantro, and avocado sauce.

11. Serve while hot.

DARK CHOCO OATMEAL WITH CARAMELIZED BANANAS

This sweet dish may taste like an indulgent dessert, but it's actually a healthy breakfast. If your child asks for something to satisfy their sweet tooth, this is an excellent choice.

TIME: 15 minutes

SERVING SIZE: 1 serving

PREP TIME: 5 minutes

COOK TIME: 10 minutes

INGREDIENTS:

- 1 tbsp dark chocolate chips
- ½ cup of rolled oats
- 1 cup of water
- 1 small banana (sliced)
- Olive oil spray

DIRECTIONS:

1. In a saucepan, add the water over medium heat and bring to a boil.

2. Add the rolled oats and turn the heat down to low.

3. Allow to simmer for about 3 to 5 minutes until the oats absorb all of the water.

4. Grease a non-stick skillet with olive oil spray over medium heat.

5. Add the banana slices and cook each side for about 3 minutes until caramelized.

6. In a bowl, add the oatmeal and top with chocolate chips and caramelized banana slices.

7. Serve while hot.

MEDITERRANEAN-STYLE BURRITO

These burritos are simple, easy, and healthy. You can make them ahead of time and store them in the refrigerator, or make them fresh even during your busy mornings.

🕐 **TIME:** 30 minutes

⚡ **SERVING SIZE:** 3 servings

PREP TIME: 15 minutes

COOK TIME: 15 minutes

INGREDIENTS:

- 1 ½ tbsp black olives (sliced)
- 1 ½ tbsp sun-dried tomatoes (chopped)
- ¼ cup of feta cheese
- ⅓ cup of refried beans (canned)
- 1 cup of baby spinach

(washed, dried)

- 3 soft tortillas
- 5 eggs
- Cooking spray
- Salsa (optional, for garnish)
- ¾ cup of sweet potato (peeled, diced)

DIRECTIONS:

1. Grease a frying pan with cooking spray over medium heat.

2. Crack the eggs into the pan and cook for about 5 minutes while scrambling.

3. Add the olives, tomatoes, and spinach, then continue cooking for about 2 minutes more.

4. Add the feta cheese and cover the pan. Continue cooking for about 3 minutes until the cheese melts.

5. Divide the refried beans between the tortillas.
6. Top each tortilla with the egg mixture.
7. Roll each tortilla to create burritos.
8. Grease a new pan with cooking spray and add the burritos.
9. Cook the burritos until lightly browned.
10. Top with salsa if desired and serve.

AVOCADO BOAT IN A HOLE

You're probably familiar with the breakfast dish where there is an egg in the middle of a slice of bread. This dish puts a healthier spin on that by adding an avocado to it.

TIME: 10 minutes

SERVING SIZE: 1 servings

PREP TIME: 2 minutes

COOK TIME: 8 minutes

INGREDIENTS:

- butter1 tbsp butter (plus more for spreading)

- 1 avocado (cut in half, pitted, and peeled)

- 1 egg

- 1 very thick slice of bread

- A handful of cheese (shredded)

- Pepper

- Salt

DIRECTIONS:

1. Use a glass or a cookie cutter to cut a hole in the middle of the slice of bread.

2. Spread butter on both sides of the bread.

3. Use a spoon to scoop some flesh out of one of the avocado halves to make room for the egg.

4. Crack the egg in a bowl then set aside.

5. In an oven-safe skillet, add the butter over medium heat.

6. Add the slice of bread and cook on one side for about 2 minutes.

7. Flip the slice of bread and place the avocado half with a hole on top.

8. Pour the egg into the hole then season with salt and pepper.

9. Cook the avocado boat for about 1 minute.

10. Take the skillet off of the stove, then sprinkle cheese all over the avocado boat.

11. Place the skillet in the oven and broil it on high for about 5 minutes.

12. Once cooked, take the skillet out of the oven and transfer the avocado boat to a plate.

13. Allow to cool for a few minutes before serving.

CLASSIC BLUEBERRY MUFFINS

There's nothing like classic blueberry muffins to start your child's day. With this recipe, you'll whip up fluffy, moist, and golden muffins that your child will surely love.

TIME: 35 minutes

PREP TIME: 13 minutes

SERVING SIZE: 12 servings

COOK TIME: 22 minutes

INGREDIENTS:

- ¼ tsp cinnamon (ground)
- ½ tsp baking soda
- ½ tsp fine sea salt
- 1 tsp baking powder
- 1 tsp white whole wheat flour
- 2 tsp vanilla extract
- ⅓ cup of extra-virgin olive oil
- ½ cup of honey
- 1 cup of blueberries (frozen or fresh)
- 1 cup of Greek yogurt (plain)
- 1 ¾ cups of white whole wheat flour
- 2 eggs (at room temperature)
- 1 tbsp raw sugar (for sprinkling)
- Cooking spray

DIRECTIONS:

1. Preheat your oven to 400°F and use cooking spray to grease a muffin tin.

2. In a bowl, add the cups of flour, baking soda, baking powder, cinnamon, and salt, then whisk together.

3. In a separate bowl, add the honey and olive oil, then whisk together.

4. Add the eggs and continue whisking.

5. While whisking, add the vanilla extract and yogurt.

6. Add the wet ingredient mixture into the bowl with the dry ingredients.

7. Use a big spoon to mix everything until just combined.

8. In a separate bowl, add 1 teaspoon of flour with the blueberries and toss to coat.

9. Fold the blueberries into the batter mixture gently.

10. Pour the batter into the muffin cups, then top each muffin with a sprinkle of raw sugar.

11. Place the muffin tin in the oven and bake the muffins for about 16 to 19 minutes. Use a toothpick to check if the muffins are cooked all the way through. Stick a toothpick into one of the muffins. If it comes out clean, they are ready.

12. Take the muffin tin out of the oven and allow the muffins to cool down before serving.

CHOCOLATE WAFFLES

Children love waffles! As you help your child transition into the vegetarian diet, you can make things easier by making dishes that they're familiar with. This is one such dish and it even has chocolate!

TIME: 35 minutes

PREP TIME: 19 minutes

 SERVING SIZE: 3 servings

COOK TIME: 14 minutes

INGREDIENTS:

- ⅓ tsp baking soda
- ⅓ tsp vanilla extract (divided)
- ½ tbsp canola oil
- 1 tbsp almonds (lightly toasted, sliced)
- 4 ½ tbsp sugar (divided)⅓ tsp baking soda
- ⅓ tsp vanilla extract (divided)
- ½ tbsp canola oil
- 1 tbsp almonds (lightly toasted, sliced)
- 4 ½ tbsp sugar (divided)

- ⅛ cup of water
- 2 ¼ cups of strawberries (cut into quarters)
- ¼ cup of cocoa (unsweetened)
- ¼ cup of Greek yogurt (plain, fat-free)
- ½ cup of buckwheat flour
- ⅔ cup of buttermilk (non-fat)
- 1 large egg (yolk only)
- 2 large eggs (whites only
- Cooking spray
- Salt

DIRECTIONS:

1. In a bowl, add the strawberries and 1 tablespoon of sugar, toss well, and allow to sit for about 30 minutes.

2. In a bowl, add the yogurt, half of the vanilla extract, and ½ tablespoon of sugar. Mix well and place in the refrigerator to chill.

3. In a separate bowl, add the cocoa, flour, salt, and baking soda, then whisk well.

4. In another bowl, add the rest of the vanilla, buttermilk, water, canola oil, and egg yolk, then continue whisking.

5. Add the mixture into the bowl with the dry ingredients and stir everything well.

6. Preheat your waffle iron.

7. In a bowl, add the egg whites and use a mixer on high to beat until the egg whites are foamy.

8. Add the rest of the sugar 1 tablespoon at a time until you form stiff and glossy peaks.

9. Scoop ¼ of the mixture into the waffle batter and fold it in gently.

10. Fold the rest of the mixture into the waffle batter.

11. Use cooking spray to grease the waffle iron.

12. Pour about ½ cup of waffle batter into the waffle iron.

13. Cook the waffle for about 4 minutes.

14. Once cooked, transfer the waffle to a plate.

15. Repeat the cooking steps for the remaining batter until you have cooked all of the waffles.

16. Before serving, top the waffles with the yogurt mixture, strawberries, and sliced almonds.

YOGURT PARFAIT

This yummy parfait contains nuts and fruits that will fill your child up and give them the energy they need to get through their morning. You can even customize the ingredients as your child wants.

TIME: 10 minutes

PREP TIME: 10 minutes

 SERVING SIZE: 2 servings

COOK TIME: no cooking time

INGREDIENTS:

- 1 tsp cinnamon
- 1 tsp honey
- 2 tbsp almonds (roughly chopped)

- ½ cup of rolled oats
- 2 plums (pitted, 1 cut in half, 1 cut into small cubes)
- 3 apricots (dried)
- 1 cup of Greek yogurt (plain, low-fat)

DIRECTIONS:

1. In a food processor, add one plum and the apricots then blend until you get a smooth texture.

2. Transfer the mixture into a bowl along with the honey, cinnamon, and yogurt then mix well.

3. In a bowl or parfait glass, layer the yogurt mixture, chopped almonds, rolled oats, and plum cubes until you use up all of the ingredients.

4. Serve immediately or chill in the refrigerator before serving.

SAVORY BREAKFAST FRITTATA

This frittata is special because it has a Mediterranean twist. It contains fresh ingredients that go well together and it will be the perfect dish to start your child's day.

TIME: 30 minutes

SERVING SIZE: 3 servings

PREP TIME: 10 minutes

COOK TIME: 20 minutes

INGREDIENTS:

- ¼ tsp salt (divided)
- 1 tsp lemon juice (freshly squeezed)
- ½ tbsp extra-virgin olive oil (divided)
- ¼ cup of basil (fresh, chopped)
- ¼ cup of pecorino Romano cheese (fresh, finely grated)
- ⅓ cup of green onions (chopped)
- ½ cup of button mushrooms (canned, sliced)
- 1 cup of baby arugula
- 4 large eggs
- Black pepper

DIRECTIONS:

1. Preheat your oven to 350°F.

2. In a bowl, add the eggs, cheese, black pepper, and half of the salt then whisk well.

3. In an oven-safe skillet, heat 1 teaspoon of oil over medium-high heat.

4. Add the mushrooms with the rest of the salt and sauté for about 5 minutes.

5. Add the onions and continue sautéing for about 2 more minutes.

6. Turn the heat down to medium and add the basil and eggs to the skillet.

7. Stir gently to mix and cook for about 5 minutes.

8. Take the skillet off the heat, place it in the oven, and bake the frittata for about 7 minutes.

9. Take the skillet out of the oven and allow the frittata to cool down for about 5 minutes.

10. In a bowl, add the arugula, lemon juice, and the rest of the oil then toss lightly. Do this while the frittata cools down.

11. Use a spatula to loosen the frittata from the skillet and transfer it to a plate.

12. Slice the frittata into three. Top each slice with arugula, and serve.

GRANOLA WITH ORANGES AND ALMONDS

This granola recipe that you can make at home has a lovely combination of honey and orange flavors. It's an excellent choice for breakfast and even as a filling snack.

TIME: 30 minutes

PREP TIME: 10 minutes

SERVING SIZE: 4 servings

COOK TIME: 20 minutes

INGREDIENTS:

- ½ tsp cinnamon (ground)

- ½ tsp fine sea salt

- 1 tsp orange zest

- ½ tbsp vanilla extract

- 1 tbsp sugar

- ¼ cup of extra-virgin olive oil

- ¼ cup of honey

- ⅓ cup of raisins (preferably golden)

- ¾ cup of almonds (raw)

- 2 cups of old-fashioned rolled oats

DIRECTIONS:

1. Preheat your oven to 350˚F and use parchment paper to line a baking sheet.

2. In a bowl, add the sugar and orange zest. Rub the sugar into the zest with your fingers until it becomes fragrant and has a bright orange color.

3. In a separate bowl, add the almonds, oats, orange zest, cinnamon, and salt, then mix well.

4. Add the honey, vanilla extract, and olive oil, then continue mixing to combine.

5. Pour the mixture into the baking sheet and use a spatula to spread it into one even layer.

6. Place the baking sheet in the oven and bake the granola for about 20 to 23 minutes. Halfway through the cooking time, stir the granola using your spatula.

7. Take the baking sheet out of the oven and allow the granola to cool down.

8. Once cool, add the raisins and mix them in. If needed, break the granola into chunks.

9. Serve immediately and store the leftovers in your refrigerator.

FANCY RASPBERRY SCONES

These scones are tasty, healthy, and oh-so fancy! You can serve them to your child for breakfast with a glass of milk and some fresh fruits. Perfect!

TIME: 35 minutes

SERVING SIZE: 6 servings

PREP TIME: 23 minutes

COOK TIME: 12 minutes

INGREDIENTS:

- ½ tsp sea salt
- ½ tbsp baking powder
- 1 tbsp cane sugar
- 1 tbsp coconut oil (chilled)
- ⅛ cup of cane sugar

- ⅛ cup of coconut oil (chilled)
- ¼ cup of coconut flour
- 1 ½ cups of whole rolled oats (preferably gluten-free)
- ⅓ cup of raspberries (sliced in half)
- ½ cup of almond milk (cold)
- ½ cup of powdered sugar

INGREDIENTS FOR THE GLAZE:
- 2 tbsp almond milk

DIRECTIONS:

1. Preheat your oven to 400°F and use parchment paper to line a baking sheet.

63

2. In a bowl, add the glaze ingredients, mix well, and set aside.

3. In a food processor, add the rolled oats and process until you get a fine flour. Measure 1 level cup and set aside the rest of the flour.

4. In a bowl, add the coconut flour, oat flour, baking powder, salt, and ⅛ cup of sugar, then mix well.

5. Add the ⅛ cup of coconut oil and use a fork to mix until you get a mixture that looks like coarse crumbs.

6. Add the almond milk then stir until well incorporated.

7. Transfer the dough onto a surface dusted with oat flour, then use your hand to knead it gently.

8. Pat down the dough and add the raspberries on one side of it.

9. Fold over the other side to cover the raspberries. Don't cover all of them; allow some raspberries to show through.

10. 10.Gently shape the dough into a round shape, then slice it **INTO 3** triangles.

11. Place the scones on the baking sheet.

12. Place the baking sheet in the oven and bake the scones for about 12 to 15 minutes.

13. Take the baking sheet out of the oven and allow the scones to cool down completely.

14. Once cool, drizzle each of the scones with the sugar glaze.

15. Serve.

QUINOA WITH APPLES AND TOASTED ALMONDS

This is another winning dish that your child will surely love. This dish is super easy to make and it's fun to eat because of all the yummy flavors and textures it has.

TIME: 15 minutes

SERVING SIZE: 2 servings

PREP TIME: 5 minutes

COOK TIME: 10 minutes

INGREDIENTS:

- ⅛ tsp cinnamon (ground)
- ⅛ tsp salt
- ½ tsp vanilla extract
- ½ tbsp canola oil
- ½ tbsp sugar

- ¼ cup of tart cherries (dried)
- ⅓ cup of almonds (slivered)
- ½ cup of Braeburn apples (sliced)
- ½ cup of quinoa (uncooked)
- 1 cup of water

DIRECTIONS:

1. Remove the lid of your Instant Pot and select 'Sauté' on the 'Normal'

mode.

2. In the inner pot, add the almonds.

3. Cook the almonds for about 2 to 3 minutes while stirring constantly.

4. Once cooked, transfer the almonds to a bowl, then set aside.

5. Add the quinoa to the Instant Pot and cook for about 1 minute while stirring frequently.

6. Add the water, canola oil, cherries, and salt, then stir well.

7. Turn off the cooker.

8. Close the lid of your Instant Pot and turn the handle to the Sealing position.

9. Press 'High Pressure' on the settings and set the time to 6 minutes.

10. After cooking on high pressure, open the cooker, add the vanilla extract, and mix well.

11. Add the apples, cinnamon, sugar, and almonds to the pot, then toss to combine.

12. Spoon the mixture into bowls and serve.

VEGGIE BREAKFAST BURRITOS

These delicious burritos are an amazing option for a healthy, savory breakfast dish. You can serve them right after making them or store these burritos in the refrigerator for on-the-go meals when you're too busy to prepare something fancy.

 TIME: 45 minutes

 SERVING SIZE: 3 servings

PREP TIME: 25 minutes

 COOK TIME: 20 minutes

INGREDIENTS:

- ⅛ tsp salt
- ½ tbsp butter (unsalted)
- 3 tbsp salsa (homemade or store-bought)
- ¼ cup of cilantro (chopped)
- ¼ cup of green onion (chopped)

- ⅓ cup of sharp cheddar cheese (shredded)
- ½ cup of black beans (canned, rinsed, drained, cooked)
- 1 small avocado (diced)
- 3 hash browns (homemade or store-bought, cooked)
- 3 large eggs
- 3 tortillas (whole-grain, warmed)

DIRECTIONS:

1. In a bowl, crack the eggs and use a fork to whisk them.

2. Add the beans and salt, then mix to combine.

3. In a skillet, add the butter over medium heat.

4. Pour the egg mixture into the skillet and cook for about 2 to 4 minutes while stirring often.

5. Transfer the eggs to a bowl, add the cheese, and mix well.

6. Add the green onion and cilantro, then continue mixing to combine.

7. Assemble the burritos. On one tortilla, add one hash brown and mash it.

8. Add 1 tablespoon of salsa, a third of the scrambled eggs, and some of the diced avocado.

9. Roll the tortilla into a burrito.

10. Repeat the assembly instructions for the other 2 burritos.

11. Serve.

MINI PIZZAS

Thinking of pizza for breakfast? Why not! Your child will surely love this! Here's one of the many recipes that will make it easier for your child to transition into their new, healthier diet.

TIME: 20 minutes

SERVING SIZE: 4 servings

PREP TIME: 10 minutes

COOK TIME: 10 minutes

INGREDIENTS:

- ¼ tsp kosher salt (divided)
- ¼ tsp pepper (divided)
- 1¼ tsp lemon zest
- 2 tsp extra-virgin olive oil
- 2 tsp lemon juice (freshly squeezed)
- ¼ cup of Parmesan cheese (grated)
- 1 cup of ricotta cheese (part-skim)
- 4 cups of baby arugula
- 1 pizza dough (store-bought, whole-wheat, at room temperature)
- 4 large eggs

DIRECTIONS:

1. Preheat your oven to 450°F and use parchment paper to line a baking sheet.

2. Divide the pizza dough into 4 balls.

3. Roll each dough ball into a circle and use a fork to pierce holes all over each mini pizza.

4. Place the mini pizza crusts on the baking sheet.

5. Place the baking sheet in the oven and bake the crusts for about 3 minutes.

6. Take the baking sheet out of the oven and flip the crusts over. Set aside.

7. In a bowl, add the lemon zest and ricotta cheese, then mix well.

8. Top each of the pizza crusts with the cheese mixture, then season with salt and pepper.

9. Crack an egg over each of the pizza crusts and then top with Parmesan cheese.

10. Place the baking sheet back in the oven and bake the pizzas for about 6 to 8 minutes.

11. In a separate bowl, add the lemon juice, olive oil, salt, pepper, and arugula, then toss to coat.

12. Once the mini pizzas are cooked, take the baking sheet out of the oven.

13. Top each mini pizza with arugula and serve.

MUESLI BOWL WITH CHERRIES AND PECANS

This is an amazing dish that your child will surely love. It's super simple to make and it will satisfy your child's sweet tooth while giving them enough energy to power through their morning.

TIME: 25 minutes

SERVING SIZE: 6 servings

PREP TIME: 10 minutes

COOK TIME: 15 minutes

INGREDIENTS:

- ¼ tsp cinnamon (ground)
- ¼ tsp salt
- ½ tbsp coconut oil (melted)
- ½ tbsp vanilla extract
- 1 tbsp maple syrup
- ¼ cup of cherries (dried, chopped)
- ½ cup of coconut flakes (unsweetened)
- ¾ cup of pecans (raw, chopped)
- 2 cups of old-fashioned rolled oats

DIRECTIONS:

1. Preheat your oven to 350 °F and use parchment paper to line a baking sheet.

2. In a bowl, add the coconut flakes, oats, pecans, cinnamon, and salt, then mix well.

3. Add the coconut oil, vanilla extract, and maple syrup, then continue mixing until well combined.

4. Pour the mixture onto the baking sheet and use a spatula to spread it out evenly.

5. Place the baking sheet in the oven and bake the muesli for about 13 to 15 minutes until the coconut flakes and oats are fragrant and lightly golden. Halfway through the cooking time, stir the muesli to cook it evenly.

6. Take the baking sheet out of the oven and allow to cool down completely before you add in the cherries.

7. Spoon the muesli into bowls and serve.

GRANOLA PARFAIT

Simple as this dish might seem, it's healthy, tasty, and filling enough for your child's first meal of the day. You can even customize the ingredients to make this dish more interesting.

TIME: 10 minutes

SERVING SIZE: 2 servings

PREP TIME: 10 minutes

COOK TIME: no cooking time

INGREDIENTS:

- ½ cup of pecan-maple granola (homemade or store-bought)

- 1 cup of blueberries

- 1 cup of yogurt (vanilla, fat-free)

DIRECTIONS:

1. Prepare all of the ingredients and the bowls [or parfait glasses].

2. Spoon each of the ingredients into the bowl, making one layer at a time. Keep creating layers until you have filled the bowl.

3. Serve immediately.

FULLY-LOADED BROWN RICE CEREAL BOWL

If you always have busy mornings, this recipe would be great for you. You can prepare it beforehand then serve it hot, warm, or even cold. After cooking, store it in your refrigerator for an on-the-go breakfast option.

TIME: 40 minutes

PREP TIME: 12 minutes

SERVING SIZE: 4 servings

COOK TIME: 28 minutes

INGREDIENTS:

- ⅛ tsp salt
- 1 tsp vanilla extract
- 2 tsp lemon zest (grated)
- 1 tbsp canola oil
- 3 tbsp sugar

- ¼ cup of heavy cream
- ½ cup of blueberries (fresh)
- ½ cup of raspberries (fresh)
- 1 cup of brown rice (uncooked, long-grain)
- 1 cup of milk (fat-free)
- 1 ½ cups of water

DIRECTIONS:

1. Open your Instant Pot then choose the 'Sauté' and 'Normal' settings.

2. Once it's hot enough, add the rice to the inner pot.

3. Cook the rice for about 3 minutes while stirring constantly.

4. Add the oil and water, close the lid, and lock it.

5. Turn the handle to the 'Sealing' position, choose the 'High Pressure' setting, and add 23 minutes for the cooking time.

6. Once cooked, turn off the cooker.

7. Spoon the rice into bowls and set aside.

8. In the cooker, add the milk, cream, sugar, and salt.

9. Choose the 'Sauté' and 'Less' settings, then cook for about 2 minutes while stirring constantly.

10. Turn the cooker off and add the vanilla extract.

11. Top each bowl with the milk mixture.

12. Top each bowl with blueberries, strawberries, and lemon zest, then serve.

CHICKPEA SCRAMBLE

This recipe is quick, healthy, and savory. It's one of those dishes that you can put together in just half an hour and have something filling for your child to eat before sending them off to school.

TIME: 30 minutes

PREP TIME: 15 minutes

SERVING SIZE: 2 servings

COOK TIME: 15 minutes

INGREDIENTS:

- 1 tsp rosemary (fresh, chopped)
- ½ tbsp extra-virgin olive oil
- 1 ½ tbsp shallots (thinly sliced)
- ¼ cup of marinara sauce (preferably low-sodium)
- ¼ cup of pecorino Romano cheese (shredded)
- 1 cup of baby spinach (fresh)
- 1 cup of chickpeas (canned, undrained)
- 1 clove of garlic (thinly sliced)
- 2 large eggs
- A dash of red pepper (crushed)
- Black pepper
- Kosher salt

DIRECTIONS:

1. In a skillet, add the oil over medium heat.

2. Add the red pepper flakes, shallots, garlic, and rosemary, then cook for about 2 minutes while stirring constantly.

3. Add the chickpeas and marinara sauce, mix, and bring to a simmer.

4. Add the baby spinach, salt, and pepper, then mix well.

5. Crack the eggs into the pan and allow all of the ingredients to simmer for about 15 minutes.

6. Cover the skillet and allow to cook for about 1 more minute.

7. Take the skillet off the heat.

8. Top the scramble with cheese and serve while hot.

HASH BROWN WAFFLES

These waffles are buttery on the inside and crispy on the outside. Who knew that you could make hash browns in your waffle iron? Genius!

TIME: 25 minutes

PREP TIME: 10 minutes

SERVING SIZE: 2 servings

COOK TIME: 15 minutes

INGREDIENTS:

- ⅛ tsp garlic powder
- ⅛ tsp onion powder
- ¾ tbsp butter (unsalted, melted)
- 1 ½ cups of russet potatoes (peeled, shredded)
- Kosher salt
- Black pepper

DIRECTIONS:

1. Preheat your waffle iron to medium-high.

2. Remove the excess liquid from the potatoes by squeezing them between paper towels.

3. In a bowl, add all of the ingredients except for the butter, then mix well.

4. Grease the waffle iron with butter and add a scoop of the potato mixture.

5. Close the waffle iron and cook the hash brown for about 12 minutes until it becomes crispy and golden brown.

6. Continue this cooking step until you have cooked all of the hash browns.

7. Serve while hot with your child's favorite dipping sauce

SAVORY EGG MUFFINS

Eggs are an important part of a healthy breakfast. Since the vegan diet includes eggs, you can include this ingredient in different types of dishes such as this one.

TIME: 25 minutes

PREP TIME: 5 minutes

SERVING SIZE: 6 egg muffins

COOK TIME: 20 minutes

INGREDIENTS:

- 1 tsp salt
- ½ cup of cheddar cheese (grated)
- 1 cup of spinach (rinsed, roughly chopped)
- 1 red bell pepper (diced)
- 2 spring onions (chopped)
- 6 eggs
- Cooking spray

DIRECTIONS:

1. Preheat your oven to 390°F and use cooking spray to grease a muffin tin.

2. In a bowl, crack the eggs one by one, add salt, and mix well.

3. Add the veggies and cheese, then continue mixing until well incorporated.

4. Pour the egg mixture into the muffin cups.

5. Place the muffin tin in the oven and bake the egg muffins for about 20 minutes.

6. Take the muffin tin out of the oven and allow the egg muffins to cool down before serving.

OATMEAL BAKE

This is a unique recipe that your child will surely enjoy. You can use either fresh or frozen blueberries in this recipe or if they aren't in season, you can use any other kind of fresh fruit.

TIME: 1 hour

PREP TIME: 10 minutes

SERVING SIZE: 8 servings

COOK TIME: 50 minutes

INGREDIENTS:

- ¾ tsp sea salt
- 1 tsp baking powder
- 1 tsp cinnamon
- 2 tbsp flaxseed (ground)
- 3 tbsp coconut oil (melted)
- 6 tbsp water (warm)
- ¼ cup of brown sugar
- ¼ cup of maple syrup
- ½ cup of almonds (slivered)
- ½ cup of blueberries
- ⅔ cup of coconut flakes
- ¾ cup of almond milk (at room temperature)
- 1 cup of strawberries (sliced)
- 2 cups of whole rolled oats
- 1 banana (chopped)
- Cooking spray

DIRECTIONS:

1. Preheat your oven to 350°F and use cooking spray to grease a baking dish.

2. In a bowl, add the warm water and flaxseed, mix well, and allow to thicken.

3. Set aside about 2 tablespoons of coconut flakes and almonds.

4. In a bowl, add the oats, baking powder, brown sugar, cinnamon, salt, the rest of the coconut flakes, and almonds. Mix well.

5. In a separate bowl, add the maple syrup, coconut oil, and almond milk, then whisk well.

6. Add the flaxseed mixture and mix well.

7. Add the wet mixture into the bowl with the dry ingredients, and continue mixing.

8. In the baking dish, add the strawberries and bananas in a single layer.

9. Top with the oat mixture and use a spatula to spread evenly.

10. 1Top the oat mixture with blueberries, coconut flakes, and almonds.

11. Place the baking dish in the oven and bake the oats for about 40 to 50 minutes.

12. Take the baking dish out of the oven and allow the oatmeal bake to cool down for about 15 minutes before you slice and serve.

RAINBOW BREKKIE BOWL

This healthy breakfast bowl is simple, easy, and customizable. You can prepare this for breakfast, lunch, or even dinner. Yes, it's that versatile!

TIME: 20 minutes

SERVING SIZE: 2 servings

PREP TIME: 10 minutes

COOK TIME: 10 minutes

INGREDIENTS:

- ⅛ tsp black pepper
- ¼ tsp kosher salt (divided)
- 1 tsp basil (fresh, chopped)
- ½ tbsp water
- 1 ½ tbsp extra-virgin olive oil (divided)
- 1 ½ tbsp apple cider vinegar
- ⅛ cup of Panko (preferably whole-wheat)
- 2 cups of baby spinach leaves
- 1 ripe avocado (peeled, pitted, sliced)
- 1 tomato (cut in half)
- 2 large eggs
- 2 slices of bacon

DIRECTIONS:

1. Preheat your broiler to high and place an oven rack at the center.

2. In a skillet, add the bacon over medium-high heat and cook for about 5 minutes until crisp.

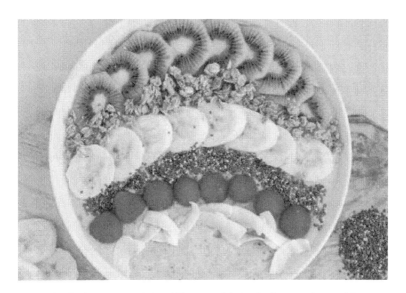

3. Take the bacon out of the skillet, crumble both slices, and set aside.

4. In the same skillet, add half of the water, a third of the oil, and the apple cider vinegar, then cook for about 30 seconds. Scrape the bottom of the pan to remove the browned bits.

5. Pour the mixture into a bowl.

6. In a separate bowl, add a third of the oil, half of the salt, Panko, and basil, then mix well.

7. Place the tomato halves on a baking sheet with the cut side facing up.

8. Top each tomato with the Panko mixture.

9. Place the baking sheet in the broiler for about 2 minutes.

10. In the skillet, add the remaining oil over medium-high heat.

11. Add the eggs into the skillet and cook for about 2 minutes.

12. Spoon the spinach into bowls.

13. Top each bowl with bacon, tomato halves, eggs, and avocado.

14. Drizzle each bowl with the vinegar mixture.

15. Sprinkle each bowl with pepper and the remaining salt.

16. Serve immediately.

HEALTHY CARROT WAFFLES

Carrots in waffles? Your child will never know how healthy this dish is. This is another easy recipe that fits into your child's diet as it features plant-based ingredients.

TIME: 25 minutes

 SERVING SIZE: 4 waffles

PREP TIME: 10 minutes

 COOK TIME: 15 minutes

INGREDIENTS:

- ½ tsp cinnamon
- 1 tsp vanilla extract
- 2 tsp baking powder
- 2 tbsp flaxseed (ground)
- 2 tbsp maple syrup
- ¼ cup of coconut oil (melted)

- 1 cup of carrots (grated)
- 2 cups of almond milk (at room temperature)
- 2 cups of whole spelt flour
- Sea salt
- Coconut cream (for serving)
- Maple syrup (for serving)

DIRECTIONS:

1. Preheat your waffle iron.

2. In a bowl, add the baking powder, cinnamon, flaxseed, flour, and salt, then mix well.

3. In a separate bowl, add the coconut oil, maple syrup, almond milk, vanilla extract, and carrots, then mix well.

4. Fold the mixture into the bowl with the dry ingredients until well combined.

5. Spoon the batter into the waffle iron and cook each waffle until cooked through and the edges are crispy.

6. Continue cooking until you have used up all of the waffle batter.

7. Serve the waffles while hot with coconut cream and maple syrup.

SUPER SMOOTHIE BOWL

Smoothies are an excellent breakfast option for children and adults alike. This recipe puts a spin on the classic smoothie by serving it in a bowl with other healthy ingredients.

TIME: 5 minutes

SERVING SIZE: 2 servings

PREP TIME: 5 minutes

COOK TIME: no cooking time

INGREDIENTS:

- 1 tbsp almond butter
- 1 cup of mixed berries (frozen)
- 4 ice cubes
- A handful of spinach
- Splashes of coconut milk (to help with the blending process)

- Blueberries (for topping)
- Coconut flakes (for topping)
- Strawberries (sliced, for topping)
- 1 tsp acai powder (optional)
- 1 tsp maple syrup (optional)

DIRECTIONS:

1. In a blender, add the coconut milk, ice cubes, almond butter, spinach, and berries, then blend well.

2. Add the maple syrup and acai powder if using and continue blending until you get the consistency you desire.

3. Pour the smoothie into bowls and add your child's favorite toppings.

4. Serve immediately.

THE EASIEST PANCAKES EVER!

Pancakes are tasty, easy, and one of the most popular breakfast dishes out there. Here's a vegetarian-friendly version of the classic pancakes for you to make for your child before school.

TIME: 20 minutes

SERVING SIZE: 2 servings

PREP TIME: 5 minutes

COOK TIME: 15 minutes

INGREDIENTS:

- 4 tbsp all-purpose flour
- 2 bananas (very ripe)
- 2 eggs (whisked)
- Cooking spray

DIRECTIONS:

1. In a bowl, add the bananas and use a fork to mash them well.

2. Add the egg and flour, then whisk everything together.

3. Use cooking spray to grease a non-stick skillet over medium-high heat.

4. Pour ½ cup of batter into the skillet and cook until the edges turn brown and bubbles pop on the surface. The cooking time depends on the size of the pancake.

5. Flip the pancake over and continue cooking for about 1 to 2 minutes more.

6. Once cooked, transfer the pancake to a plate.

7. Repeat the cooking steps until you have used up all of the pancake batter.

8. Serve the pancakes while hot with syrup, nuts, or fresh fruits.

CLASSIC FRENCH TOAST

French toast is another classic dish that will make it easier for your child to transition into the vegetarian diet. This recipe is very simple and it's even gluten-free.

TIME: 15 minutes

PREP TIME: 10 minutes

SERVING SIZE: 2 servings

COOK TIME: 5 minutes

INGREDIENTS:

- ¼ teaspoon nutmeg (freshly ground)
- 1 tsp cinnamon
- 1 tbsp maple syrup
- 1 tbsp nutritional yeast
- 2 tbsp millet flour
- 1 cup of almond milk
- 6 slices of ciabatta bread (preferably a day-old)
- A pinch of salt
- Coconut oil (for cooking)

DIRECTIONS:

1. In a bowl, add the flour, almond milk, maple syrup, cinnamon, nutmeg, nutritional yeast, and salt, then mix well.

2. Pour the mixture into a shallow dish that's wide enough for the bread to fit.

3. In a skillet, drizzle some coconut oil over medium heat.

4. Dip one of the bread slices in the milk mixture and coat both sides evenly.

5. Add the slice of bread to the skillet and cook each side for a few minutes until golden brown. The cooking time depends on the size and thickness of your bread slices.

6. Once cooked, transfer the bread slice to a plate.

7. Repeat the cooking steps until you have cooked all of the slices of bread.

8. Serve while hot with some vegan butter, fresh fruits, powdered sugar, or maple syrup.

TOFU SCRAMBLE

This is a super recipe that you can serve with toppings like avocado slices, salsa, or even fresh vegetables. It's savory, healthy, and completely plant-based.

TIME: 15 minutes

PREP TIME: 5 minutes

SERVING SIZE: 2 servings

COOK TIME: 10 minutes

INGREDIENTS:

- ⅛ tsp cumin (ground)
- ⅛ tsp turmeric (ground)
- ¼ tsp Dijon mustard
- ½ tbsp extra virgin olive oil
- 1 tbsp nutritional yeast
- ¼ cup of almond milk
- ¼ cup of yellow onion (diced)
- ¾ cup of tofu (extra-firm, patted dry, crumbled)
- 1 clove of garlic (minced)
- Black pepper
- Sea salt

DIRECTIONS:

1. In a bowl, add the almond milk, mustard, garlic, cumin, turmeric, nutritional yeast, and salt, then mix well. Set aside.

2. In a skillet, add the oil over medium heat.

3. Add the onion, season with salt and pepper, and cook for about 5 minutes until soft.

4. Add the tofu and continue cooking for about 3 to 5 minutes more.

5. Turn the heat down to low, add the milk mixture, and continue cooking for about 3 minutes more while stirring occasionally.

6. Transfer the tofu scramble into plates and serve with toppings or side dishes of your choice. Some excellent options are tomatoes, tortillas, sautéed kale or spinach, or avocado slices.

SMOKY BREAKFAST TOSTADA

If you have a tortilla at home, you can easily make this dish using any other ingredients you have in your kitchen. You can even prepare everything beforehand and have your child make their own breakfast tostada!

TIME: 15 minutes

SERVING SIZE: 2 servings

PREP TIME: 5 minutes

COOK TIME: 10 minutes

INGREDIENTS:

- 3 tsp green onions (thinly sliced)
- 2 tbsp cheddar cheese (shredded)
- 4 tbsp chipotle salsa (homemade or store-bought)
- 2 corn tortillas (whole-grain)
- 2 large eggs (fried)

DIRECTIONS:

1. Bake the tortillas at 350°F for about 8 to 10 minutes.

2. Top each tortilla with a fried egg, cheese, green onions, and salsa.

3. Serve.

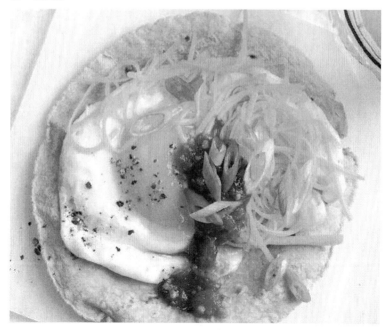

EASY CHIA PUDDING

Chia pudding is another simple dish that you can customize and even make beforehand. You can ask your child to choose which fruit to use here or follow this recipe as it is.

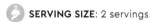 **TIME:** 5 minutes (chilling time not included)

PREP TIME: 5 minutes

SERVING SIZE: 2 servings

COOK TIME: no cooking time

INGREDIENTS:

- ⅛ tsp cinnamon
- ½ tbsp of maple syrup
- ⅛ cup of chia seeds
- ¾ cup of almond milk (you can also use coconut milk or cashew milk)
- A pinch of sea salt
- Nuts or seasonal fruit (chopped, for topping)
- ¼ tbsp lemon juice (freshly squeezed, optional)

DIRECTIONS:

1. In a bowl, add the milk, chia seeds, cinnamon, maple syrup, salt, and lemon juice if desired, then mix well.

2. Cover the bowl and place in the refrigerator for about 30 minutes to chill.

3. Take the bowl out of the refrigerator and stir the pudding.

4. Cover the bowl and place it back in the refrigerator overnight or for a minimum of 6 hours.

5. When you're ready to serve, spoon the pudding into bowls and top with your choice of nuts or fresh fruits.

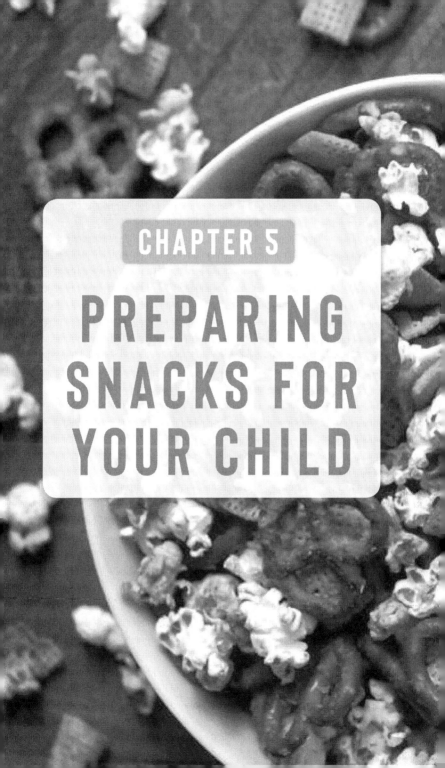

CHAPTER 5

PREPARING SNACKS FOR YOUR CHILD

We all love snacks, right? For children, snacking at least once or twice a day is a necessity, whether at school or at home. Since children are very active, they tend to burn more energy than adults, which is why they need to eat more frequently, too. You don't have to necessarily stop your child from snacking. Instead, you should teach your child to choose healthy snacks to tide them over until their next meal, that way they aren't just filling their bodies with empty calories.

THE IMPORTANCE OF SNACKING OCCASIONALLY

Although we all enjoy snacks once in a while, these mini-meals have gained a bad reputation since they are considered unnecessary. Many people believe that you should just wait until your next meal instead of consuming additional calories that might cause you to gain weight.

But the truth is, snacks are essential energy boosters that will fill in the gaps between your dedicated meal times throughout the day. By focusing on healthy foods, these snacks will help improve your health instead of hindering you from reaching your health goals. If you want to make the most out of snacks for yourself and your child, consider these important points:

- The amount should be sufficient—just enough to boost your energy without being too excessive.
- They must be high in water and fiber such as whole grains, fruits, and the like.
- Snacks that contain a combination of healthy carbs and protein are the best kinds.
- They must be low in [unhealthy] fat and sugar.
- They must be fresh, whole foods instead of packaged or processed snacks.

Snacking occasionally or as needed is essential for your health. To make sure that snacks will be healthy for your child, you should:

- Get rid of junk foods in your kitchen or at least store these unhealthy snacks somewhere hidden.
- Also, avoid buying unhealthy or non-vegetarian snack items so that you [and your child] don't end up going back to your old eating habits. As soon as you finish your stocks of snacks that don't belong to your new diet, focus on buying healthier options.
- Replace your child's sugary snacks with more nutritious options that

you have prepared yourself.
* Eat the same healthy snacks as your child so that they will feel more encouraged to snack on healthy foods.

By following these guidelines, you won't have to worry whenever your child asks for a snack at any time throughout the day.

ALL ABOUT SNACKS: MYTHS VS. REALITY

For so long, snacks have been generalized as unhealthy foods, which, as you now know, isn't always true. Through dedicated scientific discovery and research, you can differentiate myths from facts. Let's go through these quickly before you learn some healthy snacks to prepare for your child:

Does Snacking Improve the Metabolism of the Body?

Myth: Yes
Fact: Although it is a common belief that snacking frequently throughout the day can increase your metabolism, there is no solid scientific evidence that supports this.

Do Snacks Affect Your Appetite?

Myth: Yes

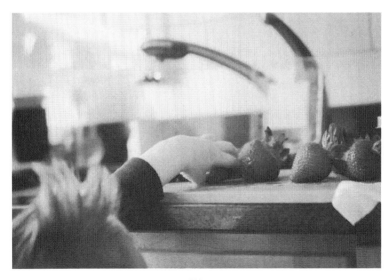

Fact: Sometimes this is true. It depends on the type of snack that you eat. For instance, if you eat a high-fiber snack right before your meal, it will reduce your appetite. But if you eat something light hours before a meal, it won't affect your appetite.

Do Snacks Increase Your Caloric Intake?

Myth: Yes
Fact: Since snacks contain calories, eating a snack will definitely increase your caloric intake. This is why it's important to eat healthy snacks so that the extra calories you consume will count.

Do Snacks Help You Lose Weight?

Myth: No
Fact: This depends on the types of snacks you eat. If you eat unhealthy snacks, they may contribute to your weight gain. On the other hand, if you consume healthy, nutrient-dense snacks, then these may help you lose weight.

Will Your Sugar Levels Increase When You Eat Snacks?

Myth: Yes
Fact: Again, this would depend on the types of snacks you eat. Some types of snacks can mess with your sugar levels while others make them more stable. To avoid any issues with your sugar levels, you must choose snacks that are low on the glycemic index.

Are Fatty Snacks Bad For Your Health?

Myth: Yes
Fact: Not necessarily. If you snack on a healthy fat source like an avocado, this is good for you. But if you snack on processed foods that are high in trans fats, these are not good for your health.

Are High-Carb Snacks Bad For You?

Myth: Yes
Fact: Again, this depends on the type of carbs you consume. If your snack contains healthy carbs like whole grains, then it's considered healthy. But you should stay away from snacks that are high in refined sugars and other unhealthy carbs.

Does Snacking Before Working Out Affect Your Performance?

Myth: Yes
Fact: This depends on the timing. If you eat a snack right before working out, it might decrease your performance. But if you eat a healthy snack at least half an hour before working out, it may improve your performance.

Does It Take a Long Time to Prepare Healthy Snacks?

Myth: Yes
Fact: Not at all. Unless you plan to make a very complex or elaborate snack, preparing healthy snacks usually takes very little time. See for yourself!

HEALTHY, TASTY, AND EASY SNACK RECIPES THAT ARE COMPLETELY PLANT-BASED

Snacks are part of any child's day. Whether at home or in school, your child needs a healthy snack to get them through to the next meal. Here are some easy snacks for you to prepare at any time of the day.

BAKED APPLE CHIPS

Children love chips! Although this snack food doesn't have a good reputation, you can make your own chips at home to make sure that they are healthier.

TIME: 40 minutes

PREP TIME: 10 minutes

SERVING SIZE: 1 serving

COOK TIME: 30 minutes

INGREDIENTS:

- 1 tsp cinnamon
- 2 apples
- Cooking spray

DIRECTIONS:

1. Preheat your oven to 350°F and use parchment paper to line a baking sheet.

2. Cut both apples in half, and then into thin slices.

3. Arrange the apple slices in a single layer on the baking sheet.

4. Coat the apple slices with oil, then sprinkle cinnamon all over them.

5. Place the baking sheet in the oven and bake the apple chips for about 30 minutes. Halfway through the cooking time, flip the apple slices over to cook them evenly.

6. Take the baking sheet out of the oven and allow the apple chips to cool down before serving.

SWEET AND CREAMY MINI BRUSCHETTA

Here's a fancy snack you can make for your child. You can mix and match the ingredients to make this dish interesting each time you serve it.

TIME: 15 minutes

PREP TIME: 15 minutes

SERVING SIZE: 20 mini bruschettas

COOK TIME: No cooking time

INGREDIENTS FOR THE SAVORY BRUSCHETTA:

- ¼ cup of basil (fresh, sliced)
- ¼ cup of cream cheese (plain)

INGREDIENTS FOR THE SWEET BRUSCHETTA:

- ¼ cup of cream cheese (plain)

- ¼ cup of pesto (homemade or store-bought)
- 1 baguette (sliced, toasted)

- ½ cup of strawberries (sliced)

DIRECTIONS:

1. Spread cream cheese on the bread slices.

2. On half of the bread slices, add a dollop of pesto and a basil leaf.

3. On the rest of the bread slices, add some strawberry slices.

4. Serve with your child's favorite drink.

CAULI-HASH BROWNS

Did you know that hash browns are not just for breakfast? You can serve them as a snack, too. Here's a healthier version of the classic dish.

TIME: 1 hour

SERVING SIZE: 3 servings

PREP TIME: 20 minutes

COOK TIME: 40 minutes

INGREDIENTS:

- ¼ tsp black pepper
- ½ tsp basil (dried)
- ½ tsp salt (divided)
- 1 tbsp olive oil
- ¼ cup of chives (fresh, thinly sliced)
- ¼ cup of Parmesan cheese
- 1 egg
- 1 small cauliflower head (coarsely grated)
- 2 cloves of garlic (minced)

DIRECTIONS:

1. Preheat your oven to 400°F and use parchment paper to line a roasting tray.

2. In a bowl, add the cauliflower and half of the salt, then toss well.

3. Set aside for about 20 minutes for the moisture to come out.

4. Line a bowl with a big towel and transfer the cauliflower into it.

5. Wrap the cauliflower with the towel and squeeze tightly to strain the liquid.

6. Transfer the strained cauliflower back into the first bowl.

7. Add the chives, cheese, olive oil, basil, garlic, egg, black pepper, and the rest of the salt, then mix well.

8. Divide the cauliflower mixture into 6 portions, shape each portion into a hash brown (you can use any shape), and place on the roasting tray.

9. Place the roasting tray in the oven and bake the hash browns for about 35 to 40 minutes. The baking time depends on the size and thickness of the hash browns.

10. Take the roasting tray out of the oven and allow the hash browns to cool down for about 15 minutes.

11. Serve with your child's favorite dipping sauce.

NACHOS WITH CASHEW CHEESE DIP

With a couple of ingredients, you can whip up a simple recipe that your child will love. The sauce you will make here is creamy, vegetarian-friendly, and absolutely scrumptious.

TIME: 10 minutes

PREP TIME: 7 minutes

SERVING SIZE: 2 servings

COOK TIME: 3 minutes

INGREDIENTS:

- ¼ tsp cumin
- ¼ tsp salt
- ¼ tsp smoked paprika
- 1 tbsp harissa
- ¼ cup of nutritional yeast

- 1 cup of cashews
- 1 cup of water
- 1 carrot (chopped)
- 1 clove of garlic
- 1 pack of tortilla chips

DIRECTIONS:

1. In a bowl, add the cashews and enough water to submerge the nuts.

2. Cover the bowl and allow to soak overnight either in the refrigerator or on the countertop.

3. When ready to use, strain the water from the cashews.

4. In a microwave-safe bowl, add the carrots with some water and then use plastic wrap to cover the bowl.

5. Place the bowl in the microwave and cook on high for about 3 to 4 minutes until the carrot chunks are fork-tender.

6. Drain the water from the bowl.

7. In a blender, add all of the ingredients except for the tortilla chips and blend until you get a smooth texture. You may add the water slowly until you get the consistency you desire.

8. Pour the nacho sauce into a bowl and serve with tortilla chips.

SALTED POPCORN CHOCOLATE BARK

This is a unique snack that you can make when your child asks you for something sweet. It's sweet, salty, and oh-so yummy!

TIME: 5 minutes

PREP TIME: 5 minutes

SERVING SIZE: 8 servings

COOK TIME: No cooking time

INGREDIENTS:

- ½ tsp coarse sea salt
- 1 cup of popcorn (popped)
- 1 ½ cups of white chocolate (chopped)
- 3 cups of dark chocolate (chopped)

DIRECTIONS:

1. Use parchment paper to line a rimmed baking sheet.

2. In a saucepan, add some water and bring to a boil.

3. In a heatproof bowl, add the dark chocolate and set it on top of the saucepan.

4. Stir the chocolate until you melt most of it.

5. Take the bowl out of the heat and continue to stir until all of the chocolate has melted.

6. Repeat the melting steps to melt the white chocolate.

7. Add half of the popcorn into the bowl with the white chocolate and mix well.

8. Pour the melted dark chocolate into the baking sheet and use a spatula to spread it evenly.

9. Drizzle the melted white chocolate over the dark chocolate.

10. Make swirls into the chocolate mixture with a knife.

11. Sprinkle the rest of the popcorn over the chocolate along with the sea salt.

12. Place the baking sheet in the oven and allow the chocolate to set for a minimum of 30 minutes.

13. Once set, take the baking sheet out of the oven and break the bark into pieces.

14. Place in an airtight container and serve whenever your child asks for something sweet.

CHEESE AND CARROT CRISPS

This simple snack contains just the right amount of savory flavors to make your child happy. The combination of carrots and gouda cheese is so perfect that you may want to make more than a single serving!

TIME: 20 minutes

SERVING SIZE: 4 servings

PREP TIME: 8 minutes

COOK TIME: 12 minutes

INGREDIENTS:

- 1 cup of carrots (shredded)
- 2 cups of Gouda cheese (shredded)

DIRECTIONS:

1. Use parchment paper to line a baking sheet.

2. Place the carrots in a paper towel or cheesecloth.

3. Wrap the carrots and squeeze out excess moisture.

4. In a bowl, add the carrots and gouda cheese, then mix well.

5. Use a spoon to scoop out mounds of the carrot mixture, place on the baking sheet, and flatten with a fork or your fingers.

6. Place the baking sheet in the oven and bake the crisps at 375°F for about 8 to 12 minutes until the cheese sizzles and the edges have turned brown.

7. Take the baking sheet out of the oven and allow the crisps to rest for about 10 minutes before transferring to a plate.

8. Serve when the crisps have cooled down completely.

CUCUMBER SUSHI

This is a refreshing dish that you can ask your child to make with you. It's simple, fresh, and colorful enough to make each piece a lot of fun to eat.

TIME: 30 minutes

SERVING SIZE: 2 servings

PREP TIME: 20 minutes

COOK TIME: 10 minutes

INGREDIENTS FOR THE TOFU:

- ¼ tsp smoked paprika
- ½ tbsp oil
- ½ block of tofu (firm)
- Black pepper
- Salt

INGREDIENTS FOR THE RICE:

- 1 tsp sugar
- ½ tbsp rice vinegar
- ¼ cup of sushi rice (cooked)
- Salt

INGREDIENTS FOR THE SUSHI:

- ⅛ orange bell pepper (thinly sliced)
- ⅛ red bell pepper (thinly sliced)
- 1 green onions
- 1 large cucumber

INGREDIENTS FOR THE SAUCE:

- ½ tsp ginger (freshly grated)
- ½ tbsp honey
- ½ tbsp lime juice (freshly squeezed)
- ½ tbsp soy sauce
- ½ tbsp water (hot)
- 1 ½ tbsp almond butter

DIRECTIONS:

1. Preheat your oven to 400°F.

2. Use a paper towel to pat the block of tofu dry, then cut it into strips, about ½-inch thick.

3. In a bowl, add the tofu and all of the seasonings, then gently rub each tofu slice to coat.

4. In an oven-safe skillet, add the oil over medium-high heat.

5. Add the tofu and cook each side for about 5 minutes until crispy.

6. Place the skillet in the oven and continue cooking for about 15 minutes more.

7. Once cooked, take the skillet out of the oven.

8. In a bowl, add the sugar, salt, and rice vinegar, then mix well.

9. Pour the mixture over the cooked rice and mix to combine.

10. In a separate bowl, add all of the ingredients for the sauce, mix well, and set aside.

11. Slice the cucumber horizontally in half and use a spoon to remove all of the seeds.

12. Spoon some rice into the cucumber and then use chopsticks to press the rice down to one side.

13. Add green onion, tofu, and bell peppers into the cucumber too. Pack all of the ingredients tightly.

14. Use a knife to slice the cucumber into "sushi" pieces.

15. Serve immediately.

CARROT AND ZUCCHINI FRITTERS

These fritters are crunchy, healthy, and they fit right into your child's new diet. If your child wants a savory snack to munch on, this is the perfect dish to prepare.

TIME: 30 minutes

SERVING SIZE: 8 fritters

PREP TIME: 15 minutes

COOK TIME: 15 minutes

INGREDIENTS:

- ½ tsp pepper
- ½ tsp salt
- ½ tsp garlic powder
- 2 tsp basil (fresh, chopped)
- ½ cup of Panko breadcrumbs (preferably whole-wheat)
- 1 cup of chickpeas (mashed)
- 1 carrot (grated)
- 1 zucchini (grated)
- 2 eggs
- Olive oil (for frying)
- Greek yogurt (plain, for serving)

DIRECTIONS:

1. Place the grated carrot and zucchini in a cheesecloth.

2. Wrap the veggies with the cheesecloth and squeeze out the excess moisture.

3. In a bowl, add the chickpeas, veggies, eggs, panko, garlic powder, basil, salt, and pepper, then mix well.

4. In a skillet, add some olive oil over medium heat.

5. Use a big spoon to scoop a portion of the mixture, shape the mixture into a patty, and add to the skillet.

6. Cook each side of the fritters for about 1 to 2 minutes until golden brown.

7. Once cooked, transfer to a plate lined with a paper towel to remove excess oil.

8. Repeat the cooking steps until you have cooked all of the fritters.

9. Serve while warm with a side of Greek yogurt for dipping.

CHOCOLATE-COVERED FRUIT KEBABS

Fruit kebabs covered in chocolate are a fun snack your child will enjoy. You can even ask them to choose which fruits to use and let them (carefully) slice and dip them in the chocolate!

 TIME: 20 minutes (chilling time not included)

PREP TIME: 12 minutes

SERVING SIZE: 3 servings

COOK TIME: 3 minutes

INGREDIENTS:

- ¼ cup of almonds (chopped)
- ½ cup of pineapple (fresh, chopped into bite-sized chunks)
- 1 cup of chocolate candy melts
- 1 banana (sliced)
- 4 strawberries (cut in half)
- 12 wooden skewers

DIRECTIONS:

1. Use parchment paper to line a baking sheet.

2. In each skewer, thread a slice of banana, a strawberry half, and a pineapple chunk.

3. Place the fruit kebab on the baking sheet.

4. Repeat the threading steps for all of the kebabs.

5. Place the baking sheet in the freezer for a minimum of 30 minutes.

6. In a bowl, add the chocolate candy melts and melt according to the instructions on the package.

7. In a shallow dish, add the almonds.

8. Take the baking sheet out of the freezer.

9. Dip one of the kebabs into the melted chocolate and then sprinkle with the chopped almonds.

10. Place the chocolate-covered kebab back onto the baking sheet.

11. Repeat the coating steps for the rest of the kebabs.

12. Place the baking sheet in the freezer for a minimum of 30 minutes before serving.

CHILLY BLUEBERRY BITES

These frozen bites will satisfy your child's sweet tooth while cooling them down, too. Make this snack as a special summer treat, or for any time of the year.

TIME: 5 minutes (chilling time not included)

PREP TIME: 5 minutes

SERVING SIZE: 4 servings

COOK TIME: No cooking time

INGREDIENTS:

- ½ cup of yogurt (vanilla-flavored, dairy-free)
- 1 cup of blueberries
- Toothpicks

DIRECTIONS:

1. Use wax paper to line a baking sheet.

2. Stick a toothpick into a blueberry, dip the blueberry in yogurt, and place on the baking sheet.

3. Repeat the coating steps until you have used up all of the blueberries.

4. Place the baking sheet in the freezer for a minimum of 1 hour.

5. Serve straight from the freezer before the yogurt melts.

RAINBOW SNACK BOX

Snack boxes are an excellent choice for children who love eating different kinds of food. This is also a great way for you to encourage your child to eat more fruits and veggies.

TIME: 10 minutes

PREP TIME: 10 minutes

SERVING SIZE: 2 servings

COOK TIME: No cooking time

INGREDIENTS:

- 1 cup of red grapes (seedless)
- 2 oranges
- 2 stalks of celery
- 10 strawberries
- Vegetarian crackers or cookies

DIRECTIONS:

1. Wash the grapes and strawberries and pat them dry.

2. Peel the oranges and separate the segments.

3. Chop the celery stalks.

4. Assemble the snack boxes by dividing all of the ingredients between them in a glass or plastic food storage container, preferably with different compartments or partitions.

5. Serve when it's time for your child to have their snack.

CRISPY KALE CHIPS

If your child isn't used to eating leafy veggies, you can encourage them by serving them in the form of chips. Since you will be making these chips at home, you can know that they will come from fresh ingredients.

TIME: 25 minutes

SERVING SIZE: 3 servings

PREP TIME: 5 minutes

COOK TIME: 20 minutes

INGREDIENTS:

- ¼ tsp garlic powder
- ¼ tsp pepper
- ¼ tsp salt
- 3 tbsp olive oil
- 3 cups of kale (chopped, hard stems removed)

DIRECTIONS:

1. Preheat your oven to 350°F and use tin foil to line a baking sheet.

2. In a bowl, add the chopped kale along with the rest of the ingredients and toss until all of the leaves are coated with oil and seasonings.

3. Transfer the kale into the baking sheet and spread them out into one layer.

4. Place the baking sheet in the oven and bake the kale chips for about 15 to 20 minutes. Halfway through the cooking time, toss the chips to cook them evenly.

5. Take the baking sheet out of the oven and allow the kale chips to cool down before serving.

SWEET QUINOA BITES

While quinoa is often used in savory dishes, you can also use this versatile ingredient for sweet treats. Here is one example of a sweet snack that will fill your child up, too.

TIME: 25 minutes

PREP TIME: 5 minutes

SERVING SIZE: 24 quinoa bites

COOK TIME: 20 minutes

INGREDIENTS:

- ⅛ tsp black pepper
- ½ tsp salt
- ½ tsp garlic powder
- 1 tsp cumin
- 1 tsp paprika
- 1 tbsp cilantro (chopped)
- ½ cup of black beans
- ½ cup of sweet potato (puréed)
- 1 ½ cups of quinoa (cooked)
- 2 eggs (whisked)
- Cooking spray

DIRECTIONS:

1. Preheat your oven to 350°F and use cooking spray to grease a mini muffin tin.

2. In a bowl, add all of the ingredients except the cooking spray and mix well.

3. Use a spoon to take a portion of the mixture and place it into the mini muffin cup.

4.   Pat the top down to flatten it slightly.

5.   Repeat the scooping steps until you have used up all of the mixture.

6.   Place the muffin tin in the oven and bake the quinoa bites for about 15 to 20 minutes.

7.   Take the muffin tin out of the oven and allow the quinoa bites to cool down.

8.   Serve to your child either chilled or warm.

BANANA TRUFFLES

Truffles are fancy and yet, they're very easy to make. Satisfy your child's sweet tooth by serving this tasty snack to them at any time of the day.

TIME: 20 minutes (freezing time not included)

PREP TIME: 20 minutes

SERVING SIZE: 4 servings

COOK TIME: No cooking time

INGREDIENTS FOR THE TRUFFLES:

- ½ tsp salt
- 2 tsp vanilla extract

INGREDIENTS FOR THE TOPPINGS:

- ⅓ cup of cocoa

- 4 tsp agave nectar
- 2 tbsp tahini
- 4 bananas (frozen, sliced)

- ½ cup of coconut (shredded)
- ½ cup of nuts (finely chopped)

DIRECTIONS:

1. In a blender, add all of the truffle ingredients and blend until you get a creamy, smooth texture.

2. Pour the mixture into 3 different containers and place them in the freezer until they turn solid.

3. When the banana mixtures have solidified, take the containers out of the freezer.

4. Add each of the toppings into separate dishes.

5. Use a mini ice cream scoop or a melon baller to scoop balls out of the banana mixtures.

6. Roll the balls into the toppings of your choice, then place them in mini cups lined up on a baking sheet. Carry out this step quickly, so the mixture doesn't melt.

7. Place the baking sheet in the freezer to firm up the truffles.

8. When ready to serve, take the truffles out of the freezer, and give them to your child for a chilly snack.

GARLIC PARM ROASTED CHICKPEAS

These chickpeas are absolutely delicious. They are crunchy, savory, and super easy to make! It's a good thing this recipe serves four, as your child will keep asking you for more.

TIME: 45 minutes

SERVING SIZE: 4 servings

PREP TIME: 5 minutes

COOK TIME: 40 minutes

INGREDIENTS:

- 1 tsp Italian seasoning
- 1 tbsp olive oil
- 2 tbsp Parmesan cheese (grated)
- 1 ¾ cups of chickpeas (canned, drained, rinsed)
- 2 cloves of garlic (minced)

DIRECTIONS:

1. Preheat your oven to 400°F and use parchment paper to line a baking sheet.

2. Dry the chickpeas carefully using paper towels.

3. In a bowl, add the chickpeas along with the rest of the ingredients.

4. Toss the chickpeas well to coat them evenly.

5. Transfer the chickpeas onto the baking sheet and spread them out into one layer.

6. Place the baking sheet in the oven and roast the chickpeas for about 35 to 40 minutes. Halfway through the cooking time, mix the chickpeas around to cook them evenly.

7. Take the baking sheet out of the oven and allow the chickpeas to cool down before serving.

CRUNCHY VEGGIE NUGGETS

This recipe is kid-friendly, simple, and it's a perfect choice for a crunchy snack. Children love crunchy foods, so you can make their diet more interesting by throwing in dishes like these once in a while.

TIME: 30 minutes

PREP TIME: 22 minutes

SERVING SIZE: 24 nuggets

COOK TIME: 8 minutes

INGREDIENTS:

- ½ tsp black pepper
- ½ tsp onion powder
- 1 tbsp canola oil
- ¾ cup of cheddar cheese (shredded)
- 1 cup of carrots (shredded)
- 1 ¼ cups of breadcrumbs (mixed with your choice of seasoning, divided)
- 3 cups of broccoli florets (steamed)
- 1 clove of garlic (minced)
- 2 eggs

DIRECTIONS:

1. In a food processor, add the carrots, broccoli, 1 cup of breadcrumbs, eggs, pepper, onion powder, and cheese, then pulse until everything is well combined. You should have a mixture that you can form into nuggets. If needed, add some water to achieve the consistency you want.

2. Scoop out a portion of the mixture, form it into a ball, and flatten slightly.

3. Repeat until you have formed many more nuggets from the rest of the mixture.

4. In a shallow dish, add the rest of the breadcrumbs.

5. Roll the nuggets in the breadcrumbs, making sure to coat them evenly.

6. Then in a skillet, add the oil and put on medium-high heat.

7. When the oil is hot enough, add the nuggets and cook each side for about 4 minutes. If needed, cook the nuggets in batches.

8. Once cooked, transfer the nuggets to a plate lined with a paper towel to absorb excess grease/oil.

9. Serve with your child's favorite dipping sauce.

CHIA OATMEAL ENERGY BITES

These energy bites are delicious, easy to make, and will give your little one enough energy to last them all afternoon. It's full of healthy ingredients, too.

TIME: 30 minutes

SERVING SIZE: 16 energy bites

PREP TIME: 10 minutes

COOK TIME: 20 minutes

INGREDIENTS:

- ½ tsp ginger (ground)
- 1 tsp cinnamon
- 1 tbsp maple syrup
- 1 tbsp vanilla extract
- 2 tbsp chia seeds
- ½ cup of almonds (slivered)
- ½ cup of applesauce (unsweetened)
- 1 ¾ cup of rolled oats
- 3 large bananas (ripe)
- 8 large strawberries (diced)

DIRECTIONS:

1. Preheat your oven to 350°F and use parchment paper to line a cookie sheet.

2. In a bowl, add the bananas and mash into a paste.

3. Add the maple syrup, applesauce, and vanilla extract, then mix well.

4. In a separate bowl, add the almonds, oats, chia seeds, ginger, and cinnamon, then mix well.

5. Add the dry ingredient mixture into the bowl with the banana mixture and mix well.

6. Fold the strawberries into the mixture.

7. Use a spoon to take portions of the mixture and drop them onto the cookie sheet.

8. Place the cookie sheet in the oven and bake the energy bites for about 20 minutes.

9. Take the cookie sheet out of the oven and allow the energy bites to cool before serving.

ZUCCHINI CHIPS

Here's another dish that uses zucchini, a very versatile ingredient to use in the vegetarian diet. Make a batch of homemade veggie chips to give your child a savory snack.

TIME: 40 minutes

SERVING SIZE: 1 serving

PREP TIME: 5 minutes

COOK TIME: 35 minutes

INGREDIENTS:

- ¼ tsp salt
- ½ tsp garlic powder

- ½ tsp pepper
- 2 tbsp olive oil
- 1 large zucchini (thinly sliced)

DIRECTIONS:

1. Preheat your 400°F and use parchment paper to line a baking sheet.

2. Arrange the zucchini slices on the baking sheet, making sure that none of the slices are overlapping with each other.

3. Brush each zucchini slice with olive oil.

4. Season the zucchini slices with garlic powder, salt, and pepper.

5. Flip the zucchini slices over and repeat the seasoning steps.

6. Place the baking sheet in the oven and bake the zucchini chips for about 25 to 35 minutes. The cooking time will depend on the thickness of the zucchini slices. Halfway through the cooking time, flip the zucchini chips over.

7. Take the baking sheet out of the oven and allow the zucchini chips to cool down before serving.

SWEET POTATO SNACK BITES

These snack bites are crunchy on the outside and soft on the inside. They even come with a delicious dip that your child will surely love.

 TIME: 55 minutes

SERVING SIZE: 4 serving

PREP TIME: 20 minutes

COOK TIME: 35 minutes

INGREDIENTS FOR THE SWEET POTATO BITES:

- ⅛ tsp garlic powder
- ¼ tsp salt
- ½ tsp cumin (ground)
- ½ tsp olive oil

INGREDIENTS FOR THE DIP:

- ¼ tsp salt
- ½ tsp paprika
- ¾ tsp cumin (ground)
- 1 tbsp tahini

- ½ tsp paprika
- ½ cup of guacamole (homemade or store-bought)
- 1 medium potato (preferably one that's long and skinny, sliced)
- A pinch of black pepper
- 1 ½ tbsp lemon juice (freshly squeezed)
- ¾ cup of black beans (canned, drained, and rinsed)
- 1 clove of garlic (minced)
- A pinch of black pepper

DIRECTIONS:

1. In a food processor, add all of the dip ingredients, and process until you get a smooth consistency. If you want a thinner consistency, you may add some water.

2. Pour the dip into a bowl and set aside.

3. Preheat your oven to 400°F.

4. On a sheet pan, add the sweet potatoes along with the spices and oil, then toss to coat all of the sweet potato slices.

5. Place the sheet pan in the oven and roast the sweet potatoes for about 35 minutes until fork-tender. Halfway through the cooking time, flip the slices over.

6. Take the sheet pan out of the oven and arrange the sweet potato bites on a plate.

7. Serve while warm with guacamole and black bean dip.

CAULIFLOWER POPCORN

Who doesn't love popcorn? This recipe puts a new twist on the classic snack as you will be using cauliflower instead of corn kernels. It's healthy and very delicious!

TIME: 25 minutes

SERVING SIZE: 1 serving

PREP TIME: 15 minutes

COOK TIME: 10 minutes

INGREDIENTS:

- ¾ cup of flour
- 1 cup of buttermilk
- 2 cups of breadcrumbs
- 1 head of cauliflower (cut into bite-sized florets)
- Black pepper
- Kosher salt
- Vegetable oil (for cooking)

DIRECTIONS:

1. In a bowl, add the flour, buttermilk, and salt, then mix well to form a smooth batter.

2. In a shallow dish, add the breadcrumbs.

3. Dredge a cauliflower floret in the buttermilk mixture, tap off excess batter, and coat with breadcrumbs.

4.   Repeat the breading steps for the rest of the florets.

5.   In a skillet, add some oil over medium heat.

6.   When the oil is hot enough, add the cauliflower florets and cook for about 2 to 3 minutes until crispy. If needed, cook the cauliflower popcorn in batches.

7.   Once cooked, transfer to a plate lined with paper towels to drain the excess oil.

8.   Sprinkle salt and pepper over the cauliflower popcorn and toss to coat.

9.   Serve while warm with your child's favorite dipping sauce.

COOKIE DOUGH SNACK BARS

For this recipe, you can make one batch of snack bars and store the rest in the refrigerator. The snack bars contain chocolate chips, which children always love.

TIME: 20 minutes (chilling time not included)

PREP TIME: 10 minutes

SERVING SIZE: 6 servings

COOK TIME: 10 minutes

INGREDIENTS:

- ¼ tsp salt
- 1 tbsp vanilla extract
- 2 tbsp coconut oil (melted)
- 2 tbsp almond milk
- ¼ cup of coconut palm sugar
- ¼ cup of raw sugar (ground)
- ½ cup of mini chocolate chips (vegan)
- ¾ cup of oat flour
- ¾ cup of almond flour

DIRECTIONS:

1. In a bowl, add the salt, onion powder, and garlic powder, then mix well. Set aside.

2. In a separate bowl, add ice water until almost full.

3. Add the sliced vegetables except for the beet slices and submerge them.

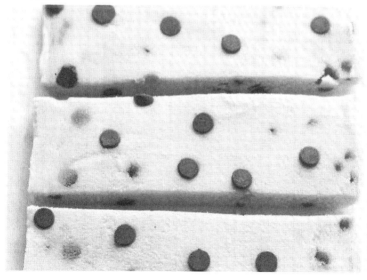

4. Add the beet slices in a smaller bowl almost filled all the way with ice water.

5. Allow the vegetable slices to soak for about 30 minutes.

6. Use paper towels to line a big baking sheet. You may also use 2 smaller baking sheets.

7. Drain the water from the sliced vegetables.

8. Arrange the sliced vegetables on the baking sheet in one layer.

9. Use paper towels to pat the vegetable slices to remove excess water.

10. Preheat your oven to 200°F.

11. Add oil to a Dutch oven or a deep pan over medium-high heat. Wait until the oil reaches a temperature of 350°F.

12. Add a batch of vegetable slices to the Dutch oven and fry for about 2 minutes until golden brown.

13. Once cooked, place the chips in a plate lined with a paper towel to drain the excess oil.

14. After draining, transfer the vegetable chips to a baking sheet, and place in the oven so the chips don't cool down.

15. Repeat the cooking steps for the remaining vegetable chips.

16. When you have cooked all of the chips, transfer them into a bowl.

17. Sprinkle the seasonings over the chips then toss lightly.

18. Serve while warm and crispy.

MIXED VEGGIE CHIPS

This unique recipe allows you to make different types of veggie chips either baked or fried. Enjoy this yummy dish with your whole family right after cooking!

TIME: 25 minutes (soaking time not included)

PREP TIME: 10 minutes

SERVING SIZE: 3 servings

COOK TIME: 15 minutes

INGREDIENTS:

- ⅛ tsp garlic powder
- ⅛ tsp onion powder
- 1 tsp kosher salt
- 1 small beet
- 1 small carrot (peeled, sliced thinly)
- 1 small parsnip (peeled, sliced thinly)
- 1 small sweet potato (peeled, sliced thinly)
- 1 small Yukon gold potato (peeled, sliced thinly)
- Canola oil (for frying)

DIRECTIONS:

1. In a bowl, add the coconut oil, coconut sugar, vanilla extract, and almond milk, then mix well.

2. Add the oat flour, almond flour, raw sugar, and salt, then continue

mixing. Taste the mixture and add more sugar if needed. If it's too sticky, add more oil or flour.

3. Fold the mini chocolate chips into the mixture.

4. Transfer the mixture onto a sheet of parchment and shape it into a rectangle with a thickness of around ½ an inch.

5. Place the parchment sheet in the refrigerator until the cookie dough sets.

6. Once set, slice the cookie dough into bars.

7. Serve the bars and place the rest in an airtight container in the refrigerator.

HOMEMADE FRUIT ROLL-UPS

Children love fruit roll-ups and if you can make them at home, you don't have to worry about any artificial ingredients. You can use other fruits for this recipe while following these basic steps.

TIME: 3 hours, 30 minutes

PREP TIME: 30 minutes

SERVING SIZE: 2 sheets of fruit roll-ups

COOK TIME: 3 hours

INGREDIENTS:

- ½ tsp cinnamon
- ⅓ cup of sugar (granulated)
- ½ cup of water
- 4 cups of apples (cored, peeled, and chopped roughly)

DIRECTIONS:

1. Preheat your oven to 170°F and use wax paper to line 2 baking sheets.

2. In a stockpot, add the apples along with the rest of the ingredients over medium heat.

3. Once the apples have become tender, mash them slightly with a potato masher and then continue cooking for 5 minutes more.

4. Pour the apple mixture into a food processor, then pulse to purée.

5.   Divide the apple purée between the 2 baking sheets, and then smooth out the mixture with a spatula.

6.   Place the baking sheets in the oven and bake the fruit roll-ups for about 3 hours until the mixtures have become slightly tacky. The cooking time will depend on the thickness of the fruit roll-ups. Every hour, swap the rack levels and rotate the baking sheets.

7.   Take the baking sheets out of the oven and allow the fruit roll-ups to cool down completely before you slice them.

8.   Serve the fruit roll-ups.

9.   Wrap the rest in wax paper, place in an airtight container, and store in the refrigerator.

SWEET POPCORN BALLS

These sweet treats are simple, easy to make, and they look super fancy. You can even ask your child to watch you make them as a fun cooking activity.

TIME: 50 minutes

SERVING SIZE: 5 servings

PREP TIME: 20 minutes

COOK TIME: 30 minutes

INGREDIENTS:

- 1 tsp apple cider vinegar
- 1 tsp vanilla extract
- ¼ cup of apple cider
- ½ cup of margarine (vegan)
- 1 cup of chocolate chips (vegan)
- 1 cup of light corn syrup
- 2 cups of sugar (granulated)
- 5 ½ cups of popcorn (popped, lightly salted)

DIRECTIONS:

1. In a bowl, add the popcorn and set aside.

2. In a deep saucepan, add the corn syrup, granulated sugar, apple cider vinegar, and margarine over medium heat.

3. Mix well and bring to a gentle boil.

4. Continue cooking while stirring regularly for about 30 minutes until the temperature reaches 300°F. Use a candy thermometer for this.

Make sure the candy reaches this temperature for the hard crack stage.

5. Regularly sweep off any sugar crystals that form around the pan using a silicone brush dipped in water. This is important to make sure that the candy solidifies and cooks properly.

6. Once the candy reaches the required temperature, take the saucepan off the heat, then stir in the vinegar and vanilla extract quickly with a wooden spoon (the same one you used for mixing).

7. Pour the mixture over the popcorn and mix well to coat the popcorn evenly. Be very careful as the candy mixture is very hot!

8. Allow the candied popcorn to cool down for about 5 to 7 minutes.

9. Scoop portions of the candied popcorn, form into balls, and place them on a wire rack to cool down completely.

10. In a microwave-safe bowl, add the chocolate chips.

11. Place in the microwave and heat on high for about 15 seconds. Take the bowl out and mix the chocolate chips.

12. Put the bowl back into the microwave and heat for about 15 seconds. Continue doing this until the chocolate chips have melted completely.

13. Place the melted chocolate into a piping bag, then drizzle it over the popcorn balls.

14. Serve when the popcorn balls have cooled completely.

APPLE CRACKERS WITH TOPPINGS

This snack is one of the quickest and easiest things you can make for your child. You can even serve it as a healthy appetizer when you host parties at home.

TIME: 5 minutes

SERVING SIZE: 10 servings

PREP TIME: 5 minutes

COOK TIME: No cooking time

INGREDIENTS:

- 3 tbsp chives (chopped)
- 3 tbsp of walnuts (lightly toasted, chopped)
- ¼ cup of celery (thinly sliced)
- ¾ cup of whipped cream

cheese (vegan)

- 3 apples (cored, sliced horizontally)
- A handful of pomegranate seeds
- 4 tbsp honey (for drizzling)

DIRECTIONS:

1. Place the apple slices on a plate and spread cheese on each of them.

2. Sprinkle each apple slice with walnuts, chives, pomegranate seeds, and celery.

3. Drizzle honey over each apple slice and serve immediately.

ASPARAGUS FRIES

While French fries made with potatoes are yummy, you can introduce this dish to your child to make them more willing to eat their greens. This is a nutritious and crunchy snack with an equally tasty dipping sauce.

TIME: 30 minutes

SERVING SIZE: 1 servings

PREP TIME: 10 minutes

COOK TIME: 20 minutes

INGREDIENTS FOR THE FRIES:

- 1 tsp pepper
- 1 tsp salt
- 1 tbsp garlic powder
- 2 tbsp oregano (dried)

- ⅓ cup of Parmesan cheese
- 1 cup of almonds (crushed)
- 1 bundle of asparagus
- 2 eggs

INGREDIENTS FOR THE DIP:

- ¼ tsp pepper
- ¼ tsp salt
- 2 tbsp chives

- 1 tbsp lemon juice (freshly squeezed)
- 1 cup of Greek yogurt (plain)

DIRECTIONS:

1. Preheat your oven to 425°F and use parchment paper to line a baking dish.

2. In a bowl, add all of the dip ingredients and mix well. Place the bowl in the refrigerator until you're ready to serve.

3. Cut off the ends of the asparagus spears and set aside.

4. In a bowl, add the Parmesan cheese, oregano, almonds, garlic powder, salt, and pepper, then mix well.

5. In a shallow dish, add the eggs and whisk well.

6. Dip an asparagus spear in the eggs and then dredge in the almond mixture.

7. Place the coated asparagus spear on the baking sheet.

8. Repeat the coating steps for the rest of the asparagus spears.

9. Place the baking sheet in the oven and bake the asparagus fries for about 15 to 20 minutes. Halfway through the cooking time, flip the asparagus spears over.

10. Take the baking dish out of the oven and allow the fries to cool down slightly before serving with dip.

BAKED BANANAS

On their own, bananas are already a wonderful snack. But this recipe in particular elevates this healthy fruit to make a tasty snack without making it too sweet.

TIME: 20 minutes

SERVING SIZE: 2 servings

PREP TIME: 5 minutes

COOK TIME: 15 minutes

INGREDIENTS:

- 1 tsp cinnamon
- 2 tbsp almond butter
- 2 bananas

DIRECTIONS:

1. Preheat your oven to 375°F.

2. Slice each of the bananas halfway through without peeling them first.

3. Widen the hole you made using your fingers.

4. Spread almond butter in the hole and sprinkle it with cinnamon. Do the same for the other banana.

5. Use aluminum foil to wrap each banana, and place them on a baking sheet.

6. Place the baking sheet in the oven and bake the bananas for about 15 minutes.

7. Take the baking sheet out of the oven and allow the bananas to cool before unwrapping and serving.

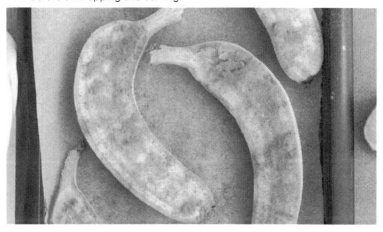

SOFT PRETZELS

There's nothing more comforting than biting into a soft, warm pretzel. This is another simple recipe you can make at home. Then you can top it with sweet or savory ingredients.

TIME: 32 minutes (rising time not included)

PREP TIME: 30 minutes

SERVING SIZE: 4 servings

COOK TIME: 12 minutes

INGREDIENTS FOR THE DOUGH:

- ½ tsp salt
- ½ tbsp active dry yeast
- ⅛ cup of white sugar (granulated)

- ½ cup of water (warm)
- 1 ¼ cups of all-purpose flour
- Cooking spray

INGREDIENTS FOR COOKING:

- ¾ tsp coarse salt

- ¼ cup of baking soda
- 3 ½ cups of water

DIRECTIONS:

1. In a bowl, add the water, sugar, salt, and yeast, then mix until all of the powdered ingredients dissolve.

2. Set aside for about 5 minutes until the mixture becomes bubbly.

3. Gradually add flour to the bowl until you form a soft dough. If needed, add more flour.

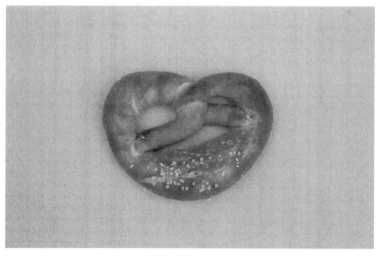

4. On a clean surface, turn out the dough and knead it for about 3 to 4 minutes until smooth and elastic.

5. Use cooking spray to grease a bowl lightly and add the dough ball to it.

6. Cover the bowl with a kitchen towel and allow the dough to rise for about 1 hour.

7. Preheat your oven to 400°F and use cooking spray to grease a baking sheet lightly.

8. In a saucepan, add the water and baking soda, then bring to a rolling boil over medium-high heat.

9. On a clean surface, turn out the dough and punch it down.

10. Divide the dough into 4 pieces and roll each piece out to make a long rope.

11. Twist the dough ropes into a pretzel shape and gently press down on the points that cross with each other so the pretzels don't unravel while cooking.

12. Drop a pretzel into the saucepan and boil it for about 30 seconds.

13. With a slotted spoon, take the pretzel out of the saucepan, and place it on the baking sheet.

14. Repeat the boiling steps for the rest of the pretzels.

15. Sprinkle each of the pretzels with coarse salt.

16. Place the baking sheet in the oven and bake the pretzels for about 11 to 12 minutes.

17. Take the baking sheet out of the oven and allow the pretzels to cool down slightly.

18. Serve with peanut butter or your child's favorite dip.

MAC & CHEESE MINI WAFFLES

This is a fun and tasty snack that combines two classics: waffles and mac & cheese. This recipe uses vegetarian-friendly ingredients so it fits right into your child's new diet.

TIME: 40 minutes

SERVING SIZE: 5 waffles

PREP TIME: 20 minutes

COOK TIME: 20 minutes

INGREDIENTS:

- 1 tbsp butter
- 1 cup of macaroni and cheese (boxed, uncooked)
- ⅛ cup of milk
- ¼ cup of breadcrumbs
- ¾ cup of cheddar cheese (shredded, divided)
- 1 egg (beaten)
- Cooking spray (for cooking)

DIRECTIONS:

1. In a pot, cook the macaroni and cheese over medium heat according to the instructions on the box. This will take around 7 to 8 minutes.

2. Drain the water and transfer the macaroni to a bowl.

3. Turn the heat down to low and in the same pot, add the butter, cheese packet (that comes in the box), and milk, then whisk well.

4. Take the pot off the heat and add the macaroni to it.

5. Add half of the cheddar cheese and mix until all of the ingredients are well-combined.

6. Add the breadcrumbs and the egg and continue mixing until well combined.

7. Preheat your waffle iron and use cooking spray to grease it lightly.

8. Pour around ½ cup of mac & cheese into the waffle iron and sprinkle cheese over it.

9. Close the waffle iron and cook the waffle for about 5 minutes until crispy and golden.

10. Once cooked, transfer the waffle to a plate.

11. Repeat the cooking steps until you have cooked all of the waffles.

12. Serve while warm.

SWEET POTATO CHIPS

These chips will awaken your child's interest since they're made from sweet potatoes. They are super crispy and flavorful. Serve them as a snack or a side dish of a plant-based meal.

TIME: 2 hours, 10 minutes

SERVING SIZE: 2 servings

PREP TIME: 10 minutes

COOK TIME: 2 hours

INGREDIENTS:

- ¼ tsp sea salt
- 2 tbsp olive oil
- 2 sweet potatoes (preferably organic)

DIRECTIONS:

1. Preheat your oven to 250°F, position a rack in the middle of the oven, and use parchment paper to line a baking sheet.

2. Rinse the sweet potatoes thoroughly and pat them dry.

3. Slice the sweet potatoes as thinly as you can using a sharp knife or a mandolin.

4. In a bowl, add the sweet potato slices, olive oil, and salt, then toss lightly to coat.

5. Arrange the sweet potato slices on the baking sheet in one layer.

6. Place the baking sheet in the oven and bake the sweet potato chips for about 2 hours. Halfway through the cooking time, flip the chips to cook them evenly. Also, check the chips every 15 minutes or so to make sure they don't burn.

7. Take the baking sheet out of the oven and allow the chips to rest and cool down for about 10 minutes before serving.

CHAPTER 6

LUNCH
THE LAST
HURDLE

At school, your child's last meal of the day will be lunch. To make sure that your child sticks with their diet even at school, you need to prepare healthy lunchboxes for them. That way, you can be sure that your child has enough energy to take on the rest of their day!

THE PENULTIMATE MEAL OF THE DAY AT SCHOOL

While at school, lunchtime is an opportunity for your child to sit with friends, hang out, and talk while enjoying their lunch. This is also the time when children check out each other's lunchboxes to see what their parents have prepared for them. Sadly, this can also be an opportunity for other children to ridicule each other's lunches.

With this in mind, you should always try to make sure that your child's lunch looks and tastes good. Just because your child is following a different diet, that doesn't mean that they should be ridiculed at school for it, right? To give you an idea of how important it is for you to pack an appealing lunch at school, here are the benefits your child will gain by indulging in healthy vegetarian lunches daily:

- It gives your child the nourishment they need to gain energy and refresh their mind for the rest of the afternoon.
- With more energy, your child's social behavior improves too. Without a proper lunch, your child might feel irritable and moody, which might cause conflicts with friends.
- It improves their focus and overall cognitive functioning. This, in turn, leads to better academic results in class.
- It helps your child handle stress and pressure more effectively. It also allows your child to make better decisions and judgments since they are more focused.

With all of these benefits to look forward to, you should definitely make an effort to prepare your child's lunches well. Fortunately, there are plenty of easy, scrumptious, and nutritious recipes you can prepare that are easy to pack in lunchboxes. When your child sees how much love and effort you put into their meals, they will always want to finish everything in their lunchbox!

PREQUEL TO A BETTER TOMORROW

Whenever children get positive feedback and impressions about their packed lunches, they will feel better about the new diet they are following. And whenever your child comes home with a smile on their face and an empty lunchbox, this means that the vegetarian dish you cooked for them has worked its magic. Apart from making sure that the meals you prepare are healthy and delicious, you should also make them presentable. That way, your child won't have to endure harsh words from other children just because of their diet.

The future of your child's vegetarian diet rests heavily upon your shoulders. You need to make sure that you choose the right dishes to pack for them. This will promote positivity in the diet along with active participation in class thanks to the energy they get from finishing their meals all the time. If you're wondering what kinds of dishes would be popular with your child, let's go through some great options now. diet.

YUMMY PLANT-BASED LUNCH RECIPES YOUR CHILD WILL LOVE

For this last chapter, you will learn how to make simple, quick, and healthy lunches for your child. Now that you know how important lunch is, especially when your child is at school, you should put in the effort to make sure that their meals are always well-prepared.

EGGPLANT BOLOGNESE

For this last chapter, you will learn how to make simple, quick, and healthy lunches for your child. Now that you know how important lunch is, especially when your child is at school, you should put in the effort to make sure that their meals are always well-prepared.

TIME: 1 hour, 30 minutes

SERVING SIZE: 3 servings

PREP TIME: 20 minutes

COOK TIME: 1 hour, 10 minutes

INGREDIENTS:

- ⅓ tsp kosher salt
- ½ tbsp oregano (fresh, finely chopped)
- 1 ½ tbsp olive oil (divided)
- ⅛ cup of heavy cream
- ⅛ cup of Parmesan cheese (grated)
- ⅛ cup of small basil leaves (fresh, loosely packed)
- ¼ cup red grape juice (unsweetened)
- ⅓ cup of shiitake mushrooms (fresh, stemmed, chopped)
- ½ cup of bucatini pasta (uncooked)
- ½ cup of yellow onion (chopped)
- ¾ cup of tomato sauce (canned)
- 1 cup of tomatoes (crushed)
- 1 small globe eggplant (chopped)
- 2 cloves of garlic (minced)

DIRECTIONS:

1. In a food processor, add the eggplant and pulse until finely shredded.

2. Transfer the eggplant into a kitchen towel, wrap it up, and squeeze out any excess liquid.

3. Transfer the eggplant to a bowl and set aside.

4. In a saucepan, add half of the oil over medium-high heat.

5. Add the onion and cook for about 3 to 4 minutes while stirring occasionally.

6. Add the mushrooms and cook for about 3 to 4 minutes until the mushrooms start turning brown.

7. Add the eggplant and cook for about 6 minutes until the eggplant starts turning brown.

8. Then, add the oregano and garlic and cook for about 1 to 2 minutes until fragrant.

9. Add the grape juice and cook for about 30 seconds while stirring the mixture and loosening any browned bits around the saucepan.

10. Add the tomatoes and the tomato sauce, then bring the mixture to a boil.

11. Once boiling, turn the heat down to low and cover the saucepan with a lid.

12. Continue cooking while stirring occasionally for about 1 hour until the vegetables are tender and the liquid has reduced slightly.

13. While the sauce simmers, cook the pasta according to the directions on the package.

14. Drain the water to avoid overcooking the pasta.

15. After simmering, add the cream into the sauce. Season with salt and stir well.

16. Spoon a portion of the pasta into a container and top with sauce.

17. Sprinkle with basil leaves and Parmesan cheese before serving.

FLATBREAD CAPRESE PIZZA

Children love pizza and it's an excellent snack to pack for lunch. This pizza is simple, delicious, and easy to make. Once you get the hang of cooking it, you can switch up the ingredients based on what your child likes.

TIME: 30 minutes

PREP TIME: 10 minutes

SERVING SIZE: 2 servings

COOK TIME: 20 minutes

INGREDIENTS:

- ¼ tsp sugar
- ½ tsp active dry yeast
- 1 tsp sea salt
- ½ cup of mozzarella cheese (fresh, cubed)
- 1 cup of grape tomatoes (sliced)
- 1 cup of water (warm)
- 2 cups of all-purpose flour
- A handful of basil leaves (fresh, sliced into ribbons)
- Cooking spray
- Extra virgin olive oil (for drizzling)

DIRECTIONS:

1. In a bowl, add the sugar, salt, yeast, and flour, then whisk well.

2. Add the water and continue mixing until you form a dough.

3. On a clean surface dusted with flour, turn out the dough.

4. Knead the dough for about 3 to 4 minutes until you form a smooth ball. Keep sprinkling more flour as needed.

5. Use a kitchen towel to cover the dough and keep it on the clean surface for about 10 minutes.

6. Preheat your oven to 425°F and use cooking spray to grease a baking sheet.

7. Roll out the dough ball into a rectangular shape, then place it on the baking sheet.

8. Drizzle olive oil all over the dough.

9. Place the baking sheet in the oven and bake the crust for about 18 to 20 minutes until crispy and golden.

10. Take the baking sheet out of the oven and place the crust on a cutting board.

11. In a bowl, add the tomatoes, mozzarella, basil leaves, salt, and a drizzle of olive oil, then mix well.

12. Pour the mixture over the crust and spread it all around.

13. Slice the pizza and serve.

VEGGIE FRIED RICE

This dish is filling, healthy, and simple to make. You can use different kinds of veggies here and even make it as colorful as you want it to be. It's also an excellent lunch box option, as your child can eat it even if it's not hot.

TIME: 35 minutes

SERVING SIZE: 3 servings

PREP TIME: 20 minutes

COOK TIME: 15 minutes

INGREDIENTS:

- ¼ tsp salt
- 1 tsp toasted sesame oil
- 3 ½ tsp avocado oil (divided)
- 1 tbsp ginger (fresh, grated)
- 1 tbsp soy sauce
- 1 cup of greens, such as baby kale or spinach
- 2 cups of brown rice (cooked)
- 2 cups of mixed veggies

like asparagus, broccoli, snow peas, cabbage, peas, or bell peppers, cut into very small pieces

- 1 small white onion (finely chopped)
- 2 carrots (finely chopped)
- 2 cloves garlic (minced)
- 2 eggs (whisked)
- 3 green onions (chopped)
- A pinch of red pepper flakes

DIRECTIONS:

1. After preparing all of the ingredients, place them within arm's reach of your stove since the cooking time is quick. Also, prepare an empty bowl near the stove to place the cooked veggies and eggs.

2. In a skillet, add some avocado oil over medium-high heat and swirl it around.

3. Add the eggs and scramble them by stirring as you cook.

4. Transfer the scrambled eggs to a bowl and use a spatula to wipe out the pan.

5. Add more avocado oil to the skillet along with the carrots and onion.

6. Cook for about 3 to 5 minutes until tender while stirring often.

7. Add the rest of the vegetables except for the greens, then season with salt.

8. Continue cooking for about 3 to 5 more minutes while stirring occasionally until all of the veggies are cooked through.

9. Transfer the cooked veggies into the bowl with the scrambled eggs.

10. Add the rest of the avocado oil to the skillet along with the garlic, red pepper flakes, and ginger, then cook for about 30 seconds while stirring occasionally.

11. Add the cooked rice, mix well, and cook for about 3 to 5 minutes.

12. Add the green onions and the green veggies, then stir to combine.

13. Add the veggies and scrambled eggs, then stir to combine.

14. Take the skillet off the heat, add the sesame oil and soy sauce, and stir well.

15. Serve while hot or pack the fried rice into your child's lunchbox.

SAVORY OATMEAL

Have you ever tried a bowl of savory oats? While we are used to eating sweet oatmeal, this savory twist on a classic meal will surely tickle your child's taste buds. It's easy to eat and you can also add different kinds of veggies to make the dish more colorful.

TIME: 30 minutes

PREP TIME: 5 minutes

SERVING SIZE: 2 servings

COOK TIME: 25 minutes

INGREDIENTS:

- ¼ tsp pepper (divided)

- ¼ tsp salt (divided)

- 1 tsp red-wine vinegar

- 1 tbsp extra-virgin olive oil (divided)

- 1 tbsp shallot (diced)

- ⅛ cup of salsa (homemade or store-bought)

- ½ cup of cheddar cheese (shredded)

- 1 cup of rolled oats (uncooked)

- 2 ¼ cups of water (divided)

- 5 cups of collard greens (chopped)

- 2 large eggs (cooked)

DIRECTIONS:

1.   In a saucepan, add half of the oil over medium heat.

2.   Add the shallots and cook for about 1 to 2 minutes while stirring

occasionally.

3. Add the oats and continue cooking for about 1 minute while stirring.

4. Add 2 cups of water and half of the salt and pepper, then bring to a boil.

5. Once boiling, turn the heat down to low.

6. Allow to simmer for about 10 to 12 minutes until creamy and smooth.

7. In a separate skillet, add the rest of the oil over medium-high heat.

8. Add the collard greens and the rest of the water, salt, and pepper, then mix well.

9. Cook for about 5 to 7 minutes while stirring occasionally.

10. Take the skillet off the heat, add the vinegar, and mix well.

11. Add the salsa and cheese into the oatmeal mixture.

12. Spoon the oatmeal into bowls, top with eggs, and serve with the collard greens.

MUSHROOM MAC & CHEESE

Have you ever tried a bowl of savory oats? While we are used to eating sweet oatmeal, this savory twist on a classic meal will surely tickle your child's taste buds. It's easy to eat and you can also add different kinds of veggies to make the dish more colorful.

TIME: 40 minutes

PREP TIME: 10 minutes

SERVING SIZE: 2 servings

COOK TIME: 30 minutes

INGREDIENTS:

- ¼ tsp kosher salt
- 2 ½ tsp thyme (fresh, chopped, and divided)
- ½ tbsp extra-virgin olive oil
- 1 tbsp all-purpose flour
- 1 tbsp panko breadcrumbs
- ¼ cup of Gruyère cheese (shredded)
- ¼ cup of mozzarella cheese

(part-skim, shredded, and divided)

- ¼ cup of shiitake mushroom caps (halved)
- ½ cup of cremini mushrooms (quartered)
- ½ cup of elbow pasta (preferably whole-wheat, uncooked)
- ¾ cup of milk (2% reduced-fat)
- 1 ½ cups of baby spinach

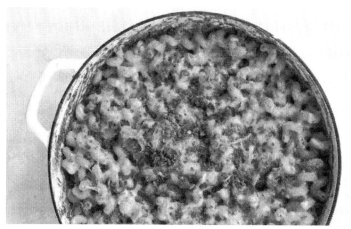

DIRECTIONS:

1. Preheat your oven to 375°F.

2. Cook the pasta according to the directions on the package.

3. Drain the water to avoid overcooking the pasta.

4. In an oven-safe skillet, add the oil over medium-high heat.

5. Add the mushrooms and cook for about 4 minutes.

6. Add half of the salt and thyme, then cook for about 2 minutes.

7. Add the flour and cook for 1 minute.

8. Add the milk, mix well, and bring the mixture to a simmer.

9. Add the cooked pasta, half of the mozzarella cheese and Gruyère cheese, then stir until the cheese melts.

10. Add the spinach and mix to combine.

11. Spread the pasta mixture evenly throughout the skillet in one layer.

12. Sprinkle the rest of the mozzarella cheese and panko on top of the pasta mixture.

13. Place the skillet in the oven and bake the mac & cheese for about 10 minutes.

14. Take the skillet out of the oven and sprinkle with the rest of the thyme.

15. Allow to cool down slightly before serving.

SWEET AND SAVORY GRILLED CHEESE

Grilled cheese sandwiches are crunchy on the outside and soft on the inside. This variety of textures is what makes them super appealing to children. This version of the classic grilled cheese is made with vegetarian-friendly ingredients without compromising on taste.

TIME: 20 minutes

SERVING SIZE: 2 servings

PREP TIME: 10 minutes

COOK TIME: 10 minutes

INGREDIENTS:

- 1 tbsp olive oil
- 1 small apple (thinly sliced)
- 1 thin slice of red onion (rings separated)
- 4 slices of cinnamon-raisin bread (preferably whole-wheat)
- 4 slices of sharp white cheddar cheese (vegan)

DIRECTIONS:

1. Place two slices of bread on a plate.

2. Top each slice with a slice of cheese, apple, onion rings, another slice of cheese, and another slice of bread.

3. Drizzle the outsides of the sandwiches with olive oil.

4. In a skillet, add the sandwiches over medium-low heat and toast each side for about 3 to 5 minutes until the cheese melts and the bread is golden brown.

5. Serve while warm.

SOBA NOODLES WITH PEANUT SLAW

This healthy Asian-style recipe has bold flavors and colorful ingredients. This is another flexible recipe as you can use different kinds of veggies for it. You can even serve the slaw separately as a side dish.

TIME: 25 minutes

SERVING SIZE: 7 servings

PREP TIME: 20 minutes

COOK TIME: 5 minutes

INGREDIENTS:

* ½ cup of soba noodles (uncooked)

* 1 cup of Brussels sprouts (ends removed)

* 1 bunch of green onions (trimmed, sliced thinly)

* 1 small purple cabbage (shredded)

* 4 carrots (peeled, shredded)

INGREDIENTS FOR THE SAUCE:

* 1 tbsp ginger (fresh, finely grated)

* 2 tbsp maple syrup

* 3 tbsp rice vinegar

* 3 tbsp soy sauce

* 3 tbsp toasted sesame oil

* ½ cup of peanut butter

* 2 cloves of garlic (minced)

INGREDIENTS FOR THE GARNISH:

* 2 tbsp peanuts (coarsely chopped)

* 1 lime (sliced)

* A handful of cilantro (coarsely chopped)

DIRECTIONS:

1. Cook the soba noodles according to the instructions on the package.

2. Drain the water, then use cold water to rinse the soba noodles.

3. In a bowl, add all of the dressing ingredients and mix well. If the

sauce is too thick, you can add some water to it. You should be able to drizzle it over the dish.

4. In a bowl, add the soba noodles and top with the veggies.

5. Drizzle the sauce over the noodles and veggies, then toss to coat everything evenly. You can enhance the flavor by letting the dish stand for at least 20 minutes before you serve it.

6. When it's time to serve, top with cilantro, peanuts, and a wedge of lime.

AVOCADO AND WHITE BEAN SANDWICHES

Sandwiches are the easiest types of lunches you can prepare for your child. For this recipe, you will create a creamy spread from plant-based ingredients for a satisfying and delicious meal. It's high in fiber, too.

TIME: 15 minutes

SERVING SIZE: 2 servings

PREP TIME: 15 minutes

COOK TIME: no cooking time

INGREDIENTS:

- ⅛ tsp pepper
- ⅛ tsp thyme (fresh, chopped)
- 1 tbsp extra-virgin olive oil
- 1 tbsp lemon juice (freshly squeezed)
- 1 cup of white beans (canned, rinsed)
- 4 cups of baby lettuce
- 1 avocado (halved, pitted, and peeled)
- 1 clove of garlic (grated)
- 4 slices of bread (preferably whole-wheat, toasted)
- 4 thin slices of sharp cheddar cheese

DIRECTIONS:

1. In a bowl, add the avocado halves and use a fork to mash them until you get a slightly chunky texture.

2. Add the beans, oil, lemon juice, thyme, garlic, and pepper, then mix well.

3. Place 2 slices of bread on a plate and spread each slice with the mixture. Top with a slice of cheese, lettuce, and another slice of bread.

4. Serve with a side of chips or homemade fries.

VEGETARIAN NOODLE SOUP

There is nothing more comforting than a bowl of soup filled with tasty and healthy ingredients. This is another Asian-style dish that you can introduce to your child. You can even whip up a big batch and store some in the freezer to take out and defrost for weeks where you need a quick meal or side dish when you're busy.

TIME: 35 minutes

SERVING SIZE: 2 servings

PREP TIME: 20 minutes

COOK TIME: 15 minutes

INGREDIENTS:

- ½ tsp soy sauce
- 1 tsp white miso
- 2 tsp toasted sesame oil (divided)
- ½ tbsp soy sauce
- ½ tbsp canola oil
- ½ tbsp ginger (fresh, grated)
- ½ tbsp mirin
- ¾ tbsp garlic (minced)
- ¼ cup of scallions (thinly sliced)

- ¼ cup of udon noodles (uncooked)
- ¼ cup of water (warm)
- ½ cup of carrots (diced)
- ¾ cup of tofu (extra-firm, drained, and cubed)
- 1 cup of cremini mushrooms (sliced)
- 2 cups of vegetable broth (preferably low-sodium)
- 1 head of baby bok choy (sliced)

DIRECTIONS:

1. Cook the soba noodles according to the instructions on the package.

2. Drain the water, put the noodles in a bowl, and set aside.

3. In a large pot, heat oil over medium heat.

4. Add the ginger and garlic, then cook for about 1 minute until fragrant.

5. Add the mirin, ½ tablespoon of soy sauce, and vegetable broth, then allow to simmer.

6. Add the carrots and mushrooms, then continue simmering for about 3 to 6 minutes.

7. Add the bok choy and continue cooking for 2 minutes more.

8. In a bowl, add the miso and warm water, then whisk until smooth.

9. Add the mixture to the pot along with the tofu and continue cooking for about 1 minute more.

10. Turn the heat off and add the scallions.

11. Use a ladle to transfer servings of the soup into bowls.

12. Drizzle with soy sauce and toasted sesame oil before serving.

QUICK AND FILLING BURRITOS

These hearty burritos will be ready in less than an hour for your child and the rest of your family. They are savory, plant-based, and an excellent choice for your child's lunch at school. You can even change some of the ingredients based on your child's preferences.

TIME: 40 minutes

SERVING SIZE: 4 servings

PREP TIME: 10 minutes

COOK TIME: 30 minutes

INGREDIENTS:

- ¼ tbsp chili powder
- ½ tsp cumin (ground)
- ½ tsp garlic (minced)
- ½ tbsp olive oil
- ¼ cup of onion (chopped)
- ½ cup of salsa (homemade or store-bought)
- ¾ cups of instant brown rice (uncooked)
- ¾ cups of water
- 1 cup of black beans (canned, rinsed, and drained)
- 1 small green pepper (diced)
- 4 flour tortillas (warmed)

DIRECTIONS:

1. In a saucepan, add the water and bring to a boil over medium heat.

2. Add the rice and bring to a boil.

3. Once boiling, turn the heat down to low and allow it to simmer for about 5 minutes.

4. Take the saucepan off the heat and allow it to sit for about 5 minutes for the rice to absorb the water.

5. In a skillet, add the oil over medium heat.

6. Add the onion and green pepper and sauté for about 3 to 4 minutes.

7. Add the garlic and continue cooking for 1 minute more.

8. Add the cumin and chili powder, then mix until well combined.

9. Add the cooked rice and beans, then cook for about 4 to 6 minutes.

10. Divide the filling between the 4 flour tortillas and top each tortilla with salsa.

11. Roll each tortilla into a burrito and serve

VEGGIE LASAGNA

This dish is becoming quite popular as more people are turning to plant-based fare. Veggie lasagna is packed with different kinds of veggies, mixed together into a classic, comforting dish. This will surely make your child a fan of vegetarian cooking.

TIME: 1 hour

PREP TIME: 30 minutes

SERVING SIZE: 8 servings

COOK TIME: 30 minutes

INGREDIENTS:

- ½ tsp salt (divided)
- 2 tbsp extra-virgin olive oil
- ¾ cups of baby spinach
- 2 cups of cottage cheese (low-fat, divided)
- 2 cups of mozzarella cheese (part-skim, freshly grated)
- 1 red bell pepper (chopped)
- 1 yellow onion (chopped)
- 1 zucchini (chopped)
- 3 large carrots (chopped)
- 9 lasagna noodles (no-boil)
- Black pepper

- **INGREDIENTS FOR THE SAUCE:**
- ¼ tsp red pepper flakes
- ½ tsp salt
- 2 tbsp extra-virgin olive oil
- ¼ cup of basil (fresh, roughly chopped)
- 3 ½ cups of tomatoes (diced)
- 2 cloves of garlic (minced)

DIRECTIONS:

1. Preheat your oven to 425°F.

2. In a skillet, add the olive oil over medium heat.

3. When hot enough, add the bell pepper, carrots, yellow onion, zucchini, and salt, then cook for about 8 to 12 minutes while stirring occasionally.

4. Add the spinach and continue cooking for about 3 minutes more until the leaves have wilted.

5. Take the skillet off the heat, then set aside.

6. In a fine colander, add the tomatoes and allow to sit for about 2 minutes to drain the excess juice.

7. Transfer the tomatoes to a food processor along with the garlic, salt, olive oil, red pepper flakes, and basil.

8. Pulse until you get a mixture with a spreadable consistency.

9. Pour the mixture into a bowl and set aside.

10. Rinse the food processor, add 1 cup of cottage cheese, and blend until smooth.

11. Pour the cottage cheese into a bowl.

12. Add the cooked veggies to the food processor and pulse until the veggies are finely chopped. Make sure not to purée the vegetables.

13. Add the chopped veggies to the bowl with the cottage cheese along with the rest of the cottage cheese. Also, add half of the salt and some pepper, then stir until well combined.

14. Scoop ½ cup of tomato sauce into a baking dish and spread it all over the bottom.

15. Top with 3 lasagna noodles.

16. Scoop half of the cottage cheese and vegetable mixture over the noodles and spread it evenly.

17. Scoop ¾ cup of tomato sauce over the cottage cheese and vegetable mixture and spread evenly.

18. Sprinkle 1 cup of mozzarella cheese over the tomato sauce.

19. Top with 3 lasagna noodles.

20. Scoop the rest of the cottage cheese and vegetable mixture and top with ½ cup of mozzarella cheese.

21. Top with 3 lasagna noodles.

22. Scoop ¾ cup of tomato sauce over the noodles, spread evenly, and sprinkle the remaining mozzarella cheese.

23. Use a sheet of foil to wrap the top of the baking dish making sure that the foil doesn't touch the cheese.

24. Place the baking dish in the oven and bake the lasagna for about 18 minutes.

25. Remove the foil, turn the baking sheet around, and continue cooking the lasagna for about 10 to 12 minutes more.

26. Take the baking dish out of the oven and allow the lasagna to cool down.

27. Serve warm.

GRILLED VEGGIE QUESADILLA

Grilling is a wonderful way to cook veggies. For this recipe, you will use grilled veggies as the filling for a healthy quesadilla. It's a great lunch option and you can also serve it for dinner. Either way, it's a tasty dish for the whole family to enjoy.

TIME: 40 minutes

PREP TIME: 25 minutes

SERVING SIZE: 2 servings

COOK TIME: 15 minutes

INGREDIENTS:

- ¼ tsp black pepper
- ¼ cup of Greek yogurt (plain, fat-free)
- ½ cup of Mexican cheese blend (shredded)
- ½ cup of pico de gallo (homemade or store-bought)
- 1 bunch of cilantro leaves (fresh)
- ¼ of a green sweet pepper
- ¼ of a red onion
- ¼ of a yellow summer squash (cut lengthwise, sliced)
- 1 corn cob (husked)
- 2 flour tortillas
- Non-stick cooking spray

DIRECTIONS:

1. Use cooking spray to lightly coat the onion, squash, corn, and pepper.

2. Grill the pepper and corn over medium heat for about 4 minutes.

3. Add the onion and grill for about 5 minutes.

4. Add the squash and grill for about 3 minutes.

5. All of the veggies should be lightly charred and tender. Turn the veggies frequently to grill them evenly.

6. Cut off the corn kernels and place them in a bowl.

7. Chop the onion, squash, and pepper coarsely, then add them to the bowl.

8. Season the veggies with black pepper and toss them lightly.

9. Spoon the veggie mixture onto the middle of the tortillas, then top with cheese.

10. Fold the tortillas in half and press down on them lightly.

11. Use cooking spray to lightly coat the tortillas.

12. Place the quesadillas on the grill and cook for about 3 to 4 minutes until crispy and golden. Halfway through the cooking time, flip the quesadillas over.

13. Serve the quesadillas with yogurt, cilantro, cheese, and pico de gallo.

VEGGIE CURRY BOWL

This vegetarian dish bursts with Indian flavors, which might be new to your child. Still, the savory flavors of this dish will surely appeal to your child's taste buds. Plus, it only takes half an hour to prepare.

TIME: 30 minutes

SERVING SIZE: 2 servings

PREP TIME: 13 minutes

COOK TIME: 17 minutes

INGREDIENTS:

- ¾ tsp olive oil
- 1 tsp curry powder
- 1 tbsp cilantro (fresh, chopped)
- ⅛ cup of yellow onion (thinly sliced)
- ¼ cup of Greek yogurt (plain, 2% reduced-fat)
- ¼ cup of vegetable broth (preferably organic)
- ½ cup of sweet potato (peeled, diced)
- ½ cup of cauliflower florets
- ¾ cup of tomatoes (canned, diced, but undrained)
- 1 cup of chickpeas (canned, rinsed, and drained)
- Salt

DIRECTIONS:

1. In a skillet, add the olive oil over medium-high heat.

2. Add the sweet potato and sauté for about 3 minutes.

3. Turn the heat down to medium and add the onion, cauliflower, and curry powder.

4. Cook for about 1 minute while stirring continuously.

5. Add the broth, chickpeas, tomatoes, and salt, then bring the mixture to a boil.

6. Once boiling, cover the skillet with a lid and allow to simmer for about 10 minutes while stirring occasionally.

7. Spoon the mixture into bowls, top with cilantro, and serve with rice.

PASTA SALAD

This dish is inspired by the classic Caprese salad, which is fresh and bright. It's the perfect summer lunch option no matter where your child is. It's super easy to make and it yields amazing results.

TIME: 20 minutes

PREP TIME: 10 minutes

SERVING SIZE: 2 servings

COOK TIME: 10 minutes

INGREDIENTS:

- 1 tsp lemon rind (freshly grated)
- 1 tbsp extra-virgin olive oil
- ⅛ cup of Romano cheese (grated)
- ⅓ cup of mozzarella cheese (fresh, cubed, and divided)
- ½ cup of farfalle (preferably whole-grain, uncooked)
- ½ cup of grape tomatoes (halved)
- ½ cup of yellow cherry tomatoes (halved)
- 1 cup of basil leaves (fresh)
- 1 clove of garlic (peeled)
- Black pepper
- Kosher salt

DIRECTIONS:

1. Cook the pasta according to the directions in the package.

2. Drain the water and transfer the pasta to a bowl.

3. In a food processor, add the oil, basil, lemon rind, salt, and pepper, then process until you get a smooth consistency.

4. Pour the mixture into the bowl with the pasta along with the tomatoes and half of the mozzarella cheese, and then toss everything to combine.

5. Top with Romano cheese and the remaining mozzarella cheese before serving.

BATTERED CAULIFLOWER RICE BOWL

Cauliflower is a very versatile ingredient that you can use in different dishes. For this recipe, you will deep-fry the cauliflower florets then coat them in sauce, and serve them over warm rice for a satisfying meal.

TIME: 45 minutes

PREP TIME: 25 minutes

SERVING SIZE: 2 servings

COOK TIME: 20 minutes

INGREDIENTS FOR THE CAULIFLOWER:

- ½ tsp baking powder
- ½ tsp salt
- ¼ cup of all-purpose flour

- ¼ cup of cornstarch
- ⅓ cup of club soda
- 2 cups of rice (cooked, hot)
- 3 cups of cauliflower florets
- Oil (for frying)

INGREDIENTS FOR THE SAUCE:

- ¼ tsp orange zest (freshly grated)
- ½ tsp ginger (fresh, grated)
- 1 tsp canola oil
- 1 tsp cornstarch
- 1 tsp sesame oil

- 1 tbsp rice vinegar
- 1 ½ tbsp soy sauce
- 1 ½ tbsp sugar
- 1 ½ tbsp vegetable broth
- ⅛ cup of orange juice
- 2 cloves of garlic (minced)
- 2 green onions (thinly sliced)

DIRECTIONS:

1. In a deep fryer, add the oil and heat to 375°.

2. In a bowl, add the cornstarch, flour, baking powder, and salt, then

mix well.

3. Add the club soda and mix well to form a thin batter.

4. Dip the cauliflower florets into the batter and add them to the deep fryer to cook for about 8 to 10 minutes.

5. Once cooked, transfer the cauliflower florets to a plate lined with a paper towel.

6. In a bowl, add the orange juice, soy sauce, rice vinegar, sugar, vegetable broth, and cornstarch, then mix well.

7. In a saucepan, add the canola oil over medium heat.

8. Add the onions, ginger, orange zest, and garlic, then cook for about 1 to 2 minutes until fragrant.

9. Add the liquid mixture into the saucepan and bring to a boil.

10. Once boiling, continue cooking for about 2 to 4 minutes more until the sauce thickens.

11. Add the cauliflower florets to the saucepan and mix well to coat.

12. Spoon the rice into bowls and top with cauliflower.

13. Serve while hot.

ROASTED LENTIL AND CAULIFLOWER TACOS

Tacos are always a fun treat at any time of the day. This vegetarian taco recipe is fresh, delicious, and crunchy. It contains different veggies that blend together perfectly. Serve this for your child's lunch at school or for a meal you will share with your family at home.

TIME: 50 minutes

SERVING SIZE: 4 servings

PREP TIME: 15 minutes

COOK TIME: 35 minutes

INGREDIENTS FOR THE TACOS:

- ½ tsp cumin (ground)
- 2 tbsp tomato paste
- 4 tbsp olive oil (divided)
- ½ cup of cilantro leaves (fresh)
- ¾ cup of brown lentils (rinsed)
- 1 cup of yellow onion (chopped)
- 2 cups of vegetable broth
- 1 large head of cauliflower (cut into florets)
- 2 cloves of garlic (minced)
- 8 small taco shells
- Salt
- Black pepper

INGREDIENTS FOR THE SAUCE:

- 1 tbsp hot sauce
- 2 tbsp lime juice (freshly squeezed)
- ⅓ cup of mayonnaise
- Black pepper
- Salt

DIRECTIONS:

1. Preheat your oven to 425°F.

2. In a bowl, add the cauliflower florets, 3 tablespoons of oil, salt, and pepper, then toss to coat.

3. Arrange the seasoned cauliflower florets on a baking sheet in one layer.

4. Place the baking sheet in the oven and roast the cauliflower florets for about 30 to 35 minutes. Halfway through the cooking time, toss the cauliflower florets.

5. Once cooked, take the baking sheet out of the oven and set aside.

6. In a pot, add the remaining olive oil over medium heat.

7. Add the garlic, onion, and salt, then sauté for about 5 minutes.

8. Add the cumin and tomato paste, then continue sautéing for another minute while stirring continuously.

9. Add the vegetable broth and lentils, then turn the heat up to medium-high.

10. Bring the mixture to a simmer and cook for about 40 to 45 minutes. If needed, add more vegetable broth so the lentils don't dry up.

11. Once the lentils are cooked through and tender, drain off the excess liquid, cover the pot with a lid, and set aside.

12. In a bowl, add all of the sauce ingredients and whisk well to combine.

13. Spoon the lentils into one of the taco shells, then top with roasted cauliflower, sauce, and cilantro.

14. Repeat the assembling steps for the remaining tacos.

15. Serve immediately. If you want to pack this dish for your child's lunch, pack the ingredients separately to avoid sogginess, then teach your child how to assemble the tacos come lunch so they can add in the fillings to the shells then.

VEGETARIAN CHILI

Chili is another classic dish that you can cook without meat. This recipe gives you a smoky twist to chili. Serve it with rice, tortilla chips, or any other side dish your child wants for lunch.

TIME: 1 hour

PREP TIME: 20 minutes

SERVING SIZE: 3 servings

COOK TIME: 40 minutes

INGREDIENTS:

- ½ tsp oregano (dried)
- ¾ tsp smoked paprika
- 1 tsp cumin (ground)
- 1 tsp lime juice (freshly squeezed)
- 1 tbsp chili powder
- 1 tbsp cilantro (fresh, chopped)
- 1 tbsp extra-virgin olive oil
- 1 cup of pinto beans (canned, rinsed, and drained)
- 1 cup of vegetable broth
- 1 ¾ cups of black beans (canned, rinsed, and drained)
- 1 ¾ cups of tomatoes

(canned, diced, with the juices)

- 1 bay leaf
- 1 celery stalk (chopped)
- 1 small carrot (chopped)
- 1 small red bell pepper (chopped)
- 1 small red onion (chopped)
- 2 cloves of garlic (minced)
- Salt
- Avocado slices (for garnish)
- Cheddar cheese (for garnish, shredded)
- Cilantro (for garnish)
- Sour cream (for garnish)
- Tortilla chips (for garnish)

DIRECTIONS:

1. In a large pot, add the olive oil over medium heat.

2. When it's hot enough, add the bell pepper, onion, celery, carrot, and some salt.

3. Cook for about 7 to 10 minutes while stirring occasionally.

4. Add the chili powder, oregano, cumin, garlic, and smoked paprika, then cook for about 1 minute while stirring continuously.

5. Add the tomatoes with the juice, pinto beans, black beans, bay leaf, and vegetable broth.

6. Stir well and bring to a simmer while stirring occasionally.

7. Continue stirring while simmering gently for about 30 minutes. If needed, turn the heat down to low.

8. Take the pot off the heat, find the bay leaf, and remove it.

9. Take 1 cup of the chili and place it in a blender.

10. Blend the chili until you get a smooth texture, then add the blended chili back into the pot. Be careful with this step as steam will come out while you are blending.

11. Add the cilantro and vinegar to the pot, then mix to combine. If needed, add more salt too.

12. Ladle portions of chili into bowls and serve with your choice of garnish.

HEALTHY VEGGIE WRAPS

Veggie wraps are easy to make and super fun to eat. You can change up the ingredients for this recipe by asking your child what veggies they want to add. You can even ask your child to help you make this dish!

TIME: 15 minutes

SERVING SIZE: 2 servings

PREP TIME: 10 minutes

COOK TIME: 5 minutes

INGREDIENTS:

- ¼ tsp black pepper (divided)
- ⅓ cup of goat cheese (crumbled)
- ¾ cups of hummus (homemade or store-bought)
- 1 cup of baby kale and spinach leaves
- 1 large orange bell pepper, seeded and thinly sliced
- 2 flour tortillas (preferably whole-wheat)
- Cooking spray

DIRECTIONS:

1. Spread the hummus over the tortillas, leaving some space around the edges.

2. Add some kale and spinach leaves along with half of the bell pepper, black pepper, and goat cheese.

3. Roll up the flour tortillas tightly.

4. Use cooking spray to grease a skillet lightly over medium-high heat.

5. Add the wraps to the skillet and cook each side for about 2 minutes until all sides are lightly browned.

6. Serve while warm.

RAINBOW QUINOA SALAD

This salad is colorful, nutritious, and easy to make. You can serve this salad right after making it, for either your child's lunch at school, or even as leftovers straight from the refrigerator. It tastes great no matter how you serve it!

TIME: 30 minutes (cooling time not included)

PREP TIME: 15 minutes

SERVING SIZE: 4 servings

COOK TIME: 15 minutes

INGREDIENTS FOR THE SALAD:

- ½ cup of grape tomatoes (halved)
- ½ cup of quinoa (uncooked, rinsed)
- 1 cup of baby spinach (fresh, thinly sliced)
- 1 cup of water

- 1 green onion (chopped)
- 1 small cucumber (seeded, chopped)
- 1 small sweet orange pepper (chopped)
- 1 small sweet yellow pepper (chopped)

INGREDIENTS FOR THE DRESSING:

- 1 tsp ginger (fresh, minced)
- 2 tsp honey
- ½ tbsp lime zest (freshly grated)

- 1 tbsp olive oil
- 1 ½ tbsp lime juice (freshly squeezed)
- Salt

DIRECTIONS:

1. In a saucepan, add the water and bring to a boil over medium heat.

2. Add the quinoa, cover the saucepan with a lid, turn the heat down to low, and simmer for about 12 to 15 minutes until the quinoa absorbs the liquid.

3. Take the saucepan off the heat and use a fork to fluff the quinoa.

4. Transfer the quinoa to a bowl and allow to cool completely.

5. In a separate bowl, add all of the dressing ingredients, and whisk together well.

6. When the quinoa has cooled completely, add the tomatoes, cucumber, spinach, green onion, and pepper into the bowl.

7. Pour the dressing into the bowl and toss everything well.

8. Place the bowl in the refrigerator to chill before serving.

CHINESE-STYLE CRISPY NOODLES

Asian-style recipes are perfect for plant-based diets. This is a fun dish your child will love as it combines amazing flavors with the crunchy texture of the noodles. Just make sure to separate the noodles from the sauce when you pack this dish in your child's lunchbox.

TIME: 50 minutes

PREP TIME: 20 minutes

SERVING SIZE: 2 servings

COOK TIME: 30 minutes

INGREDIENTS FOR THE NOODLES:

- 1 tbsp canola oil (divided)
- ¼ cup of Chinese noodles (uncooked)
- ¼ cup of cilantro (fresh, coarsely chopped)
- ¼ cup of mint (fresh, coarsely chopped)

INGREDIENTS FOR THE SAUCE:

- ½ tsp ginger (freshly grated)
- ¼ tbsp lime zest (freshly grated)
- ½ tbsp soy sauce

- ½ cup of cabbage (shredded)
- 1 cup of carrots (shredded)
- ½ block of tofu (extra-firm, drained)
- ¼ cup of peanuts (unsalted, roasted, and chopped, for topping)
- 2 scallions (thinly sliced, for topping)
- ½ lime (sliced, for serving)
- ½ tbsp toasted sesame oil
- 1 tbsp honey
- 1 tbsp lime juice (freshly squeezed)
- ⅛ cup of natural peanut butter (creamy)

DIRECTIONS:

1.   In a bowl, add all of the sauce ingredients, mix well, and set aside.

2.   Preheat your oven to 400°F and use paper towels to line a baking sheet.

3.   Cut the block of tofu into cubes then arrange them on the baking sheet in one layer.

4.   Cover the tofu cubes with another paper towel.

5.   Press down on the paper towel gently to absorb the excess liquid from the tofu cubes.

6.   Remove all of the paper towels and discard them.

7.   In an oven-safe skillet, add half of the canola oil over medium-high heat.

8.   Add the tofu and cook for about 5 minutes until all cubes are lightly browned.

9.   Place the skillet in the oven and bake the tofu for about 10 to 15 minutes until crispy.

10. Take the skillet out of the oven and set aside.

11. In a pot, add the water and bring to a boil.

12. Add the Chinese noodles and cook for about 3 minutes.

13. Drain the water from the pot.

14. In a skillet, add the remaining canola oil over medium-high heat.

15. Add the Chinese noodles and press them down into the bottom of the skillet to create a thin layer of noodles.

16. Cook the noodles for about 3 to 5 minutes until crispy and lightly browned.

17. Flip the layer of noodles over and continue cooking for another 3 to 5 minutes.

18. Transfer the crispy noodles to a plate.

19. Top with tofu cubes, cabbage, carrots, mint, and cilantro.

20. Drizzle the sauce all over the noodles and vegetables.

21. Sprinkle with scallions and peanuts.

22. Serve with lime slices.

AVOCADO AND CHEESE QUESADILLAS

The avocado in this dish makes it super filling and nutritious. This is a plant-based dish where you can add other ingredients to make it even more filling. Serve this as a heavy snack or a light lunch paired with a piece of fruit.

TIME: 20 minutes

SERVING SIZE: 2 servings

PREP TIME: 10 minutes

COOK TIME: 10 minutes

INGREDIENTS FOR THE SALAD:

- ½ tbsp canola oil
- 1 ½ tbsp cilantro (fresh, minced)
- ½ cup of pico de gallo (homemade or store-bought)
- 1 cup of Mexican cheese blend (shredded)
- 1 small avocado (ripe, peeled, and thinly sliced)
- 8 corn tortillas

DIRECTIONS:

1. Sprinkle the tortillas with some water to make them moist.

2. Use canola oil to grease a griddle over medium heat.

3. Add 4 tortillas to the griddle and sprinkle cheese over them.

4. When some of the cheese has melted, top the tortillas with avocado slices, cilantro, pico de gallo, and the rest of the tortillas.

5. Cook each side for about 3 to 4 minutes until the cheese melts and the tortillas are lightly browned.

6. Serve while warm.

SWEET POTATO AND BLACK BEAN ENCHILADAS

Mexican-style dishes are very popular on plant-based diets because the flavors work well with plant-based ingredients. These enchiladas are tasty and they will serve as a hearty meal for your child to enjoy on their lunch break.

TIME: 1 hour, 20 minutes

PREP TIME: 20 minutes

SERVING SIZE: 4 servings

COOK TIME: 1 hour

INGREDIENTS:

- ¼ tsp black pepper
- ¼ tsp salt
- ½ tsp chili powder
- ½ tsp cumin (ground)
- 1 tbsp water
- 2 tbsp lime juice (freshly squeezed)
- 2 tbsp sour cream
- ¼ cup cilantro (fresh, chopped)
- ¼ cup of red onion (chopped)
- ½ cup of feta cheese (crumbled)
- ½ cup of green chilies (canned, diced)
- 2 cups of Monterey Jack cheese (grated, divided)
- 1 ¾ cups of black beans (canned, rinsed, and drained)
- 2 cups of salsa verde (mild, homemade or store-bought)
- 2 cloves of garlic (minced)
- 2 sweet potatoes
- 10 corn tortillas

DIRECTIONS:

1. Preheat your oven to 400°F and use parchment paper to line a baking sheet.

2. Cut the sweet potatoes in half vertically, then use olive oil to coat all of the flat sides.

3. Place the sweet potato halves on the baking sheet with the flat sides facing down.

4. Place the baking sheet in the oven and bake the sweet potatoes for about 30 to 35 minutes until they are cooked through and tender.

5. Take the baking sheet out of the oven but don't turn it off yet.

6. In a separate baking dish, pour ½ cup of salsa verde and spread it all over the bottom.

7. In a bowl, add the black beans, feta cheese, green chilies, garlic, lime juice, cumin, chili powder, salt, pepper, and half of the Monterey Jack cheese, then mix well.

8. Use a spoon to scoop out the flesh of the sweet potato halves.

9. Add the sweet potato flesh to a bowl and discard the skins.

10. Use a fork to mash the sweet potato flesh, add it to the bowl with the cheese mixture, and mix well. If needed, add more salt and pepper.

11. Warm one tortilla and scoop ½ a cup of filling in the middle.

12. Roll the tortilla and place it on the baking dish where you baked the sweet potatoes.

13. Repeat the assembling steps for the rest of the tortillas.

14. Top the tortillas with the rest of the Monterey Jack cheese and salsa verde.

15. Place the baking sheet in the oven and bake the enchiladas for about 30 to 35 minutes until the cheese turns golden and the sauce bubbles.

16. Take the baking sheet out of the oven and allow the enchiladas to cool down for about 5 minutes.

17. In a bowl, add the water and sour cream, then mix well.

18. Drizzle the sauce over the enchiladas before serving.

SWEET AND SAVORY LUNCH BOXES

This simple lunch box contains different ingredients to make your child's lunchtime fun and interesting. You can customize the ingredients of this recipe and even allow your child to assemble their own lunch to bring to school.

TIME: 5 minutes

PREP TIME: 5 minutes

SERVING SIZE: 1 serving

COOK TIME: No cooking time

INGREDIENTS:

- 1 tbsp fruit jam
- 1/8 cup of cheddar cheese (cubed)
- 1/8 cup of goat cheese
- 1/4 cup of smoked almonds
- 1/2 apple (sliced)
- 1/2 carrot (peeled, cut into sticks)
- 6 small crackers (preferably whole-grain)

DIRECTIONS:

1. Place the jam and the almonds in small containers and add them to the lunchbox.

2. Arrange the rest of the ingredients around the small containers.

3. Place the lunchbox in the refrigerator to chill until ready to serve.

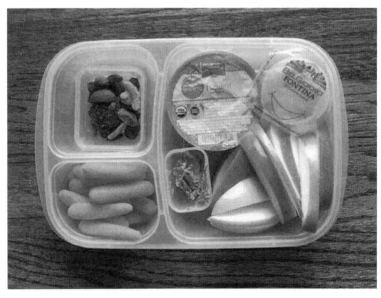

HEARTY ITALIAN-STYLE SOUP

A bowl of this soup will surely fill up your child and make them feel super satisfied. Just make sure that when you pack this for your child's lunch at school, you store it in a leak-proof, airtight container.

TIME: 30 minutes

SERVING SIZE: 3 servings

PREP TIME: 5 minutes

COOK TIME: 25 minutes

INGREDIENTS:

- 1 tsp thyme (fresh, minced)
- ½ tbsp olive oil
- 1 tbsp parsley (fresh, minced)
- ½ cup of tomato sauce
- 1 cup of navy beans (canned, rinsed, and drained)
- 1 cup of vegetable broth
- 1 carrot (chopped)
- 1 celery rib (chopped)
- 1 small onion (chopped)
- 1 small potato (peeled, cubed)
- 1 small zucchini (chopped)

DIRECTIONS:

1. In a pot, add the oil over medium-high heat.

2. Add the carrot and potato, then cook for about 3 minutes.

3. Add the zucchini, celery, and onion, then cook for about 3 to 4 minutes until the veggies are tender and crisp.

4. Add the rest of the ingredients and bring the mixture to a boil.

5. Once boiling, turn the heat down to medium, cover the pot, and simmer for about 12 to 15 minutes.

6. Ladle soup into bowls and serve while warm.

THAI-STYLE CABBAGE LEAF WRAPS

This dish is fresh, savory, and crunchy thanks to the cabbage leaves. Serve this dish as a light lunch and pair it with a bowl of sliced fruits or a small cup of noodles. You can also add more cabbage wraps to your child's lunchbox for a more filling meal.

TIME: 1 hour

PREP TIME: 30 minutes

SERVING SIZE: 4 servings

COOK TIME: 30 minutes

INGREDIENTS FOR THE TOFU:

- 1 tbsp olive oil
- 1 tbsp soy sauce

INGREDIENTS FOR THE MANGO SALSA:

- ¼ teaspoon salt
- 1 ½ tbsp lime juice (freshly squeezed)

INGREDIENTS FOR EVERYTHING ELSE:

INGREDIENTS FOR THE SAUCE:

- 1 ½ tbsp lime juice (freshly squeezed)
- 2 tsp toasted sesame oil
- 2 tbsp apple cider vinegar

- 2 tsp cornstarch
- 1 block of tofu (extra-firm, preferably organic)

- ⅓ cup of cilantro leaves (fresh, chopped)
- 1 red bell pepper (chopped)
- 2 mangoes (ripe, diced)
- 4 green onions (chopped)
- 2 tbsp peanuts (chopped)
- 1 small head of cabbage
- 2 tbsp honey
- 2 tbsp soy sauce
- ⅓ cup peanut butter (creamy)
- 2 cloves of garlic (minced)

DIRECTIONS:

1. Preheat your oven to 400°F and use parchment paper to line a baking sheet.

2. Slice the block of tofu into 3 pieces and place the slices on a plate lined with paper towels.

3. Put a paper towel on top of one tofu slice and then place another tofu slice on top, alternating between the two until you have stacked all your tofu slices with paper towels in between, separating each one.

4. Add more paper towels to the pile of tofu slices, then place a skillet on top of the pile to squeeze out the water from the slices of tofu.

5. While the tofu drains, make the sauce and the salsa. In a bowl, add all of the sauce ingredients and mix well. You can add more water if it's too thick. Set aside.

6. In a bowl, add all of the mango salsa ingredients and mix well. Set aside.

7. Remove the paper towels from the pile of tofu, then cut each tofu slice into 4 pieces.

8. In a bowl, add the soy sauce and 1 tablespoon of olive oil, then mix well.

9. Drizzle the mixture over the tofu cubes and toss well.

10. Add 1 teaspoon of cornstarch to the bowl, then continue to toss to coat the tofu cubes.

11. Place the tofu on the baking sheet in one layer, making sure that there are spaces in between.

12. Place the baking sheet in the oven and bake the tofu for about 30 to 35 minutes until the tofu is golden and crisp. Halfway through the cooking time, toss the tofu cubes.

13. When the tofu is cooked, take the baking sheet out of the oven and allow the tofu to cool down slightly.

14. Cut off the bottom part and the stem of the cabbage, then pull 8 leaves off one at a time.

15. Divide the mango salsa equally among the cabbage leaves.

16. Top with tofu, crushed peanuts, and sauce.

17. Wrap and serve.

TOMATO SOUP WITH GRILLED CHEESE SQUARES

Grilled cheese sandwiches go perfectly with tomato soup, so this combination is definitely a winner. You can even prepare this dish beforehand and freeze it so that you have a quick go-to option when you're too busy in the morning.

TIME: 30 minutes

SERVING SIZE: 2 servings

PREP TIME: 18 minutes

COOK TIME: 12 minutes

INGREDIENTS:

- ⅛ tsp oregano (dried)
- ⅛ tsp pepper
- ¼ tsp basil (dried)
- ¼ tsp salt
- 1 tsp brown sugar
- 1 tsp canola oil
- 2 tbsp butter (vegan)
- ⅛ cup of celery (finely chopped)
- ⅛ cup of onion (finely chopped)
- ¾ cup of water
- 1 ¾ cups of tomatoes (canned, diced, and undrained)
- 4 slices of bread (lightly toasted)
- 4 slices of cheese
- Basil (fresh and minced, for topping)

DIRECTIONS:

1. In a saucepan, add the oil over medium-high heat.

2. Add the celery and onion, then cook for about 2 to 4 minutes until tender.

3. Add the rest of the ingredients and bring the mixture to a boil.

4. Once boiling, turn the heat down to low and allow it to simmer for about 10 minutes.

5. While the soup simmers, prepare the grilled cheese sandwiches.

6. Butter all sides of all slices of bread.

7. Place two slices of bread on a plate.

8. Top each one with a slice of cheese, then another slice of bread.

9. In a skillet, toast the sandwiches for about 3 to 4 minutes on each side until the cheese melts.

10. Place the sandwiches on a cutting board and cut each of them into quarters. Set aside.

11. When the soup is done, pour it into a blender.

12. Puree the soup, then return it to the saucepan for about 3 minutes until heated through.

13. Pour the soup into bowls and top with minced basil.

14. Serve with grilled cheese sandwich squares.

OPEN-FACE WILD RICE PATTY SANDWICHES

This is a unique dish that will surprise your child. It's made with wild rice patties instead of beef patties, but it's so delicious that your child will feel happy that they tried it. Although the dish takes some time to make, it will definitely be worth the extra time and effort.

TIME: 1 hour, 45 minutes

PREP TIME: 45 minutes

SERVING SIZE: 3 servings

COOK TIME: 1 hour

INGREDIENTS:

- ⅛ tsp basil (dried)
- ¼ tsp white pepper
- ⅓ tsp crushed red pepper
- ⅓ tsp garlic (granulated)
- ½ tsp parsley (fresh, finely chopped)
- ¾ tsp butter
- ¾ tsp cumin (ground)
- ¾ tsp extra-virgin olive oil
- ¾ tsp garlic (minced)
- ½ tbsp red-wine vinegar
- 1 tbsp extra-virgin olive oil
- ⅛ cup of jarred roasted red peppers (bottled, rinsed, and finely chopped)

- ¼ cup of cereal squares (crushed)
- ¼ cup of mushrooms (finely chopped)
- ¼ cup of parsley (fresh, finely chopped)
- ¼ cup of pepper Jack cheese (sliced)
- ⅓ cup of mayonnaise (reduced-fat)
- ½ cup of wild rice
- 1 cup of water
- 1 large egg (lightly beaten)
- 1 large onion (thinly sliced)
- 3 slices of bread (whole-wheat, toasted)
- Cooking spray

DIRECTIONS:

1. In a saucepan, add the water and bring to a boil over medium heat.

2. Add the wild rice and cook for about 20 to 30 minutes until tender while stirring occasionally.

3. Drain the water and allow the rice to cool down slightly.

4. In a skillet, add the butter and ¾ teaspoon of olive oil over medium heat.

5. Add the onions and cook for about 35 to 40 minutes until they turn a deep golden brown.

6. Preheat your oven to 350°F, arrange the oven racks on the upper and middle parts of the oven, and then use cooking spray to grease a baking sheet.

7. In a bowl, add the granulated garlic, cumin, white pepper, and red pepper flakes, then mix well.

8. Add the rice, cereal, mayonnaise, mushrooms, eggs, and ¼ cup of parsley, then mix well.

9. Divide the mixture into 3 portions, shape each portion into a patty, and place on the baking sheet.

10. Place the baking sheet on the middle rack and bake the patties for about 30 minutes until lightly brown and firm.

11. In a bowl, add the peppers, minced garlic, vinegar, basil, and the remaining oil and parsley, then whisk well.

12. Turn on your oven's broiler setting to high.

13. Transfer the baking sheet to the top rack and top each patty with a slice of cheese.

14. Broil the patties for about 1 to 3 minutes until the cheese melts.

15. Take the baking sheet out of the oven.

16. Place the slices of bread on a plate.

17. Top each slice of bread with a patty, onions, and drizzle with the vinaigrette.

18. Serve while warm.

PO'BOY SANDWICHES

This sandwich is fresh, fun, and super tasty. Here, you will even learn how to make your own sauce to level up this sandwich and make it one of your child's favorite dishes. Serve this at home or pack it in your child's lunchbox for a unique kind of meal.

TIME: 30 minutes

SERVING SIZE: 2 servings

PREP TIME: 10 minutes

COOK TIME: 20 minutes

INGREDIENTS FOR THE SANDWICHES:

- ¾ tbsp Creole seasoning (you may also use Cajun seasoning)
- ⅓ cup of panko breadcrumbs
- 2 cups of cauliflower florets
- 1 egg (lightly beaten)
- 2 lettuce leaves

INGREDIENTS FOR THE DRESSING:

- ½ teaspoon paprika

- 2 soft baguette pieces (lightly toasted)
- 2 tomato slices
- 4 pickle slices
- Zest of 1 lemon
- Chives (chopped, for topping)
- Extra-virgin olive oil (for drizzling)
- Lemon wedges (for serving)
- ½ tbsp mustard
- ¼ cup of mayonnaise
- 1 clove of garlic (minced)

DIRECTIONS:

1. Preheat your oven to 400°F and use parchment paper to line a baking sheet.

2. In a shallow dish, add the Creole seasoning, lemon zest, and panko, then mix well.

3. Crack the egg in a bowl and beat it lightly.

4. Dip one of the cauliflower florets in the egg, dredge in the breadcrumb mixture, then place on the baking sheet.

5. Repeat the breading steps for the rest of the cauliflower florets.

6. Drizzle the cauliflower florets with olive oil.

7. Place the baking sheet in the oven and bake the cauliflower florets for about 20 minutes until golden brown and crispy.

8. Take the baking sheet out of the oven and prepare to assemble the sandwiches.

9. In a bowl, add the sauce ingredients and mix well. Set aside.

10. Spread the sauce over the baguette pieces.

11. Top each sandwich with lettuce leaves, tomato and pickle slices, and the baked cauliflower.

12. Top with chives and serve the sandwiches with lemon wedges and an extra side of sauce.

BAGUETTE PIZZA

If you tell your child that you're packing pizza for their lunch, they will surely jump for joy. Although this pizza looks different, it's still pretty amazing. Pair it with a fresh salad for a perfect meal in school.

TIME: 35 minutes

PREP TIME: 15 minutes

SERVING SIZE: 3 servings

COOK TIME: 20 minutes

INGREDIENTS:

- ¼ tsp Italian seasoning
- 1 tsp olive oil
- ⅓ cup of basil leaves (fresh, thinly sliced, and divided)
- ½ cup of mushrooms (fresh, sliced)
- ¾ cup of mozzarella cheese

(part-skim, shredded)

- 1 clove of garlic (minced)
- 1 French baguette (sliced in half lengthwise)
- 1 onion (sliced)
- 2 small tomatoes (sliced)
- A pinch of pepper
- A pinch of salt

DIRECTIONS:

1. Preheat your oven to 400°F.

2. In a skillet, add the oil over medium-high heat.

3. Add the onions and mushrooms, then sauté for about 4 to 5 minutes

until tender.

4. Add the seasonings and garlic, then cook for 1 minute while stirring.

5. Place the baguette halves with the flat side facing up on a baking sheet.

6. Sprinkle half of the cheese and basil over the baguette halves.

7. Top with cooked mushroom and onions, sliced tomatoes, and the rest of the cheese.

8. Place the baking sheet in the oven and bake the baguette pizzas for about 10 to 15 minutes until the cheese melts.

9. Take the baking sheet out of the oven and sprinkle the remaining basil over the baguette pizzas before serving.

SPAGHETTI SQUASH BOWLS

Spaghetti squash is an amazing ingredient you can use for a variety of different dishes. For this recipe, you will create a delicious, colorful dish that's good for your child. You can change up the ingredients if you want to as well.

TIME: 1 hour

PREP TIME: 10 minutes

SERVING SIZE: 2 servings

COOK TIME: 50 minutes

INGREDIENTS FOR THE SPAGHETTI SQUASH:

- 1 tbsp olive oil
- 1 spaghetti squash (cut in half, seeded)
- Black pepper
- Salt

INGREDIENTS FOR THE SLAW:

- ½ tsp olive oil
- 2 tbsp lime juice (freshly squeezed)
- ¼ cup of cilantro (fresh, chopped)
- ¼ cup of green onions (chopped)
- ½ cup of black beans (canned, rinsed, and drained)
- 1 cup of purple cabbage (thinly sliced, roughly chopped)
- 1 small red bell pepper (chopped)
- Salt

INGREDIENTS FOR THE SALSA:

- ½ tbsp lime juice (freshly squeezed)
- ¼ cup of cilantro (fresh)
- ⅓ cup of salsa verde (mild, homemade or store-bought)
- 1 small avocado (ripe, diced)
- 1 small clove of garlic (roughly chopped)
- Crumbled feta (optional, for topping)

DIRECTIONS:

1. Preheat your oven to 400°F and use parchment paper to line a baking sheet.

2. Place the spaghetti squash halves on the baking sheet with the flat side facing up.

3. Drizzle olive oil over both of the squash halves and rub it all over them.

4. Season the insides with salt and pepper, then turn the halves over.

5. Place the baking sheet in the oven and roast the spaghetti squash for about 40 to 60 minutes. The cooking time will depend on the size of the spaghetti squash halves. You'll know it's done when you can pierce the flesh with a fork easily.

6. In a bowl, add all of the slaw ingredients and mix well. Set aside for the veggies to absorb the flavors.

7. In a food processor, add all of the salsa ingredients and blend until you get a smooth texture.

8. Pour the salsa into a bowl and set aside.

9. Take the baking sheet out of the oven.

10. Use a fork to fluff up the spaghetti squash's flesh.

11. Top each spaghetti squash bowl with half of the slaw and half of the salsa.

12. Sprinkle each bowl with cilantro, pepper, and feta cheese if desired.

13. Serve while hot.

CONCLUSION: LIVING THE VEGETARIAN LIFESTYLE

A vegetarian diet can potentially change your life in so many ways. Now that you know everything there is to know about this diet and how you can help your child follow it, you can start planning your own vegetarian diet journey. As promised at the beginning of this book, we explored all the fundamentals of the vegetarian diet, especially in terms of how it can eventually be your child's new approach to eating.

We began by defining the vegetarian diet itself, along with its benefits and potential drawbacks to give you a big-picture look at what to expect. We also discussed the importance of this diet, the controversies surrounding it, and how you can supplement this diet to avoid nutrient deficiencies, which are the most common risks of plant-based diets like this one. Next, we discussed the practical side of this diet to help you encourage your child to follow the diet correctly. From helping your child adjust to the diet at home and in school to learning how to store your plant-based foods well, this book has equipped you with a lot of practical tips and information, especially in the second chapter of this book.

The next chapter focused on how you will help your child actually start the diet. You learned about your roles as a parent, your child's

roles, some activities to make their transition more enjoyable, and even a number of potential danger signs to look out for. All of these are important topics as you need them to start planning your child's vegetarian diet. Lastly, we included a bunch of amazingly healthy, tasty, and easy recipes you can start cooking for your child now, covering breakfast, lunch, and snacks. This highly detailed and comprehensive collection of recipes ensures that you always have a variety of different, interesting meals to choose from, that way things don't get repetitive or boring. This is certainly essential if you and your family like to try new things.

From start to finish, this book has provided you with valuable information about the vegetarian diet. Now, all you have to do is apply everything you have learned to your life. It will take some time and a lot of patience, but if you can successfully help your child follow this diet, you will notice not only their health improve, but also teach them to develop lifelong habits that will have a tremendous impact on their life and the planet.

REFERENCES

6.6: Diseases Involving Proteins. (2016, July 29). Medicine LibreTexts. https://med.libretexts. org/Bookshelves/Nutrition/Book%3A_An_Introduction_to_Nutrition_(Zimmerman)/06%3A_ Proteins/6.06%3A_Diseases_Involving_Proteins

Adams, A. (2021, January 22). Make Your Own Vegan Soft Pretzels at Home. The Spruce Eats. https://www.thespruceeats.com/dairy-free-soft-pretzels-1000567

Andrews, B. (2020, June). Rice Patty Melts. EatingWell. https://www.eatingwell.com/ recipe/280136/rice-patty-melts/

Barnard, N. D. (2017, May 15). How to Raise Healthy Vegetarian Children. Vegetarian Times. https:// www.vegetariantimes.com/health-nutrition/raising-veg-kids/

Becoming a Vegetarian (for Teens). (2014). Kidshealth.org. https://kidshealth.org/en/teens/ vegetarian.html

Bilow, R. (2015, January 19). How to Make Flavorful, Healthy Vegetarian Meals. Bon Appétit. https:// www.bonappetit.com/test-kitchen/cooking-tips/article/vegetarian-cooking-ideas

Blair Wyckoff, W. (2019). Raising Vegetarian Kids? Here Are Some Pointers. Npr. https://www.npr. org/templates/story/story.php?storyId=129137062

Bond, S. (2016, January 25). Baked Cheese Crisps (with Hidden Carrot!). Live Eat Learn. https:// www.liveeatlearn.com/gouda-cheese-crisps-with-carrots/

Bond, S. (2017, January 20). Almond Butter Baked Bananas. Live Eat Learn. https://www. liveeatlearn.com/almond-butter-baked-bananas/

Bond, S. (2018a, June 9). Tofu Stuffed Cucumber Sushi Roll. Live Eat Learn. https://www. liveeatlearn.com/tofu-stuffed-cucumber-sushi-rolls/

Bond, S. (2018b, October 17). Health(ier) Chocolate Bark with Salted Popcorn. Live Eat Learn. https://www.liveeatlearn.com/healthy-chocolate-bark-with-salted-popcorn/

Bond, S. (2019a, February 20). Vegetarian Meal Prep Snack Boxes. Live Eat Learn. https://www. liveeatlearn.com/meal-prep-snack-boxes/

Bond, S. (2019b, July 15). Frozen Blueberry Bites. Live Eat Learn. https://www.liveeatlearn.com/ frozen-blueberry-bites/

Bond, S. (2020a, February 7). Strawberry Chia Oatmeal Cookies (GF + Vegan). Live Eat Learn. https://www.liveeatlearn.com/strawberry-chia-oat-bites/

Bond, S. (2020b, April 29). The BEST Cashew Queso! (Vegan). Live Eat Learn. https://www. liveeatlearn.com/vegan-cashew-queso/

Bonom, D. (2013, January). Mushroom Frittata Recipe. MyRecipes. https://www.myrecipes.com/ recipe/mushroom-frittata-0

Bonom, D. (2016, June). Pesto Pasta Salad with Tomatoes and Mozzarella Recipe. MyRecipes. https://www.myrecipes.com/recipe/pesto-pasta-salad-tomatoes-mozzarella

Booth, S. (2017, July 7). Can Vegetarian Food Fuel Your Kids? WebMD; https://www.webmd.com/ parenting/raising-fit-kids/food/features/should-kids-go-vegetarian

Bourassa, L. (2010, February 22). Disadvantages of a Vegetarian Diet. LIVESTRONG; https://www. livestrong.com/article/85540-disadvantages-vegetarian-diet/

Broadfoot, R. (n.d.-a). Apple Chips Recipe by Tasty. Tasty. https://tasty.co/recipe/apple-chips

Broadfoot, R. (n.d.-b). Zucchini Chips Recipe by Tasty. Tasty. https://tasty.co/recipe/zucchini-chips

Brody, J. E. (2017, June 5). Feeding Young Minds: The Importance of School Lunches. The New York Times. https://www.nytimes.com/2017/06/05/well/feeding-young-minds-the-importance-of-school-lunches.html

Brown, M. (n.d.). Satisfying Tomato Soup. Taste of Home. https://www.tasteofhome.com/recipes/ satisfying-tomato-soup/

Caland, L. (n.d.). Tomato Baguette Pizza. Taste of Home. https://www.tasteofhome.com/recipes/tomato-baguette-pizza/

Cazorla-Lancaster, Y. (2021). What are the Benefits of Plant-Based? Veggie Fit Kids. https://www.veggiefitkids.com/benefits

CBS News. (2011, June 15). 14 myths about healthy eating. CBS News. https://www.cbsnews.com/pictures/14-myths-about-healthy-eating/10/

Cebula, T. (2017, March). Waffle Iron Hash Browns Recipe. MyRecipes. https://www.myrecipes.com/recipe/waffle-iron-hash-browns

Children's Health Team. (2018, January 11). Is a Vegan Diet Safe for Growing Children? Health Essentials from Cleveland Clinic; https://health.clevelandclinic.org/is-a-vegan-diet-safe-for-growing-children/

Cleveland Clinic. (2020). Anemia: Symptoms, Types, Causes, Risks, Treatment & Management. Cleveland Clinic. https://my.clevelandclinic.org/health/diseases/3929-anemia

Cookie and Kate. (2014, July 22). Thai Mango Cabbage Wraps. Cookie and Kate. https://cookieandkate.com/thai-mango-cabbage-wraps/

Cookie and Kate. (2015, May 1). Roasted Cauliflower and Lentil Tacos. Cookie and Kate. https://cookieandkate.com/roasted-cauliflower-and-lentil-tacos/

Cookie and Kate. (2017b, August 24). Cherry Pecan Muesli Recipe. Cookie and Kate. https://cookieandkate.com/cherry-pecan-muesli-recipe/

Cookie and Kate. (2017c, November 22). Black Bean Sweet Potato Enchiladas. Cookie and Kate. https://cookieandkate.com/black-bean-sweet-potato-enchiladas/

Cookie and Kate. (2017d, December 7). Best Vegetable Lasagna Recipe. Cookie and Kate. https://cookieandkate.com/best-vegetable-lasagna-recipe/

Cookie and Kate. (2018a, January 20). Orange & Almond Granola Recipe. Cookie and Kate. https://cookieandkate.com/orange-almond-granola-recipe/

Cookie and Kate. (2018b, February 24). Vegetarian Breakfast Burritos Recipe. Cookie and Kate. https://cookieandkate.com/vegetarian-breakfast-burritos-recipe/

Cookie and Kate. (2018c, May 29). Peanut Slaw with Soba Noodles. Cookie and Kate. https://cookieandkate.com/peanut-soba-noodle-slaw-recipe/

Cookie and Kate. (2019a, April 20). Healthy Blueberry Muffins Recipe. Cookie and Kate. https://cookieandkate.com/healthy-blueberry-muffins/

Cookie and Kate. (2019b, April 20). Homemade Vegetarian Chili. Cookie and Kate. https://cookieandkate.com/vegetarian-chili-recipe/

Cookie and Kate. (2020, November 16). Healthy Breakfast Casserole Recipe. Cookie and Kate. https://cookieandkate.com/healthy-breakfast-casserole-recipe/

Dave. (2019, September). Healthy Yogurt Parfait. Hurrythefoodup.com. https://hurrythefoodup.com/fruity-yogurt-parfait/

Dave. (2020, November 19). Breakfast Egg Muffins. Hurry the Food Up. https://hurrythefoodup.com/low-carb-egg-breakfast-muffins/

Davidson, A. (2018, October 4). 6 Snacking Myths You Need to Stop Believing. Stylist. https://www.stylist.co.uk/life/recipes/6-snacking-myths-you-need-to-stop-believing/229114

Department of Health & Services. (2020) Breakfast. Better Health. https://www.betterhealth.vic.gov.au/health/healthyliving/breakfast#:~:text=Breakfast%20is%20often%20called%20

Diabetic Living Magazine. (n.d.). Grilled Vegetable Quesadilla. EatingWell. https://www.eatingwell.com/recipe/266915/grilled-vegetable-quesadilla/

Digestive Disorders. (2014, March 29). The Benefits of a Vegetarian Diet. UPMC HealthBeat; https://share.upmc.com/2014/03/benefits-of-a-vegetarian-diet/

Dolge, A. (2019, August). 5 Risky Refrigerator Mistakes to Avoid. EatingWell. https://www.eatingwell.com/recipe/274137/white-bean-avocado-sandwich/

Dolgo, A. (2021). Eggplant Bolognese Recipe. MyRecipes. https://www.myrecipes.com/recipe/eggplant-bolognese-0

Donofrio, J. (2013, April 15). Vegan French Toast Recipe. Love and Lemons. https://www.loveandlemons.com/vegan-french-toast/

Donofrio, J. (2016a, January 20). Easiest Chia Pudding Recipe. Love and Lemons. https://www.loveandlemons.com/chia-pudding/

Donofrio, J. (2016, April 13). Vegan Scones with Raspberries Recipe. Love and Lemons. https://www.loveandlemons.com/vegan-scones/

Donofrio, J. (2016b, May 12). Berry Superfood Smoothie Bowl Recipe. Love and Lemons. https://www.loveandlemons.com/berry-superfood-smoothie-bowl/

Down to Earth. (2019, January 30). Top 10 Reasons for Going Veggie. Down to Earth Organic and Natural. https://www.downtoearth.org/go-veggie/top-10-reasons

Driskill, M. (2021). Skillet Mushroom Mac and Cheese Recipe. MyRecipes. https://www.myrecipes.com/recipe/skillet-mushroom-mac-cheese

Editors of Epicurious. (2020, March 18). How to Freeze Fruits and Vegetables. Epicurious. https://www.epicurious.com/expert-advice/how-to-freeze-summer-fruits-and-vegetables-article

Eswaran, V. (2018, December 18). Vegetarianism is Good for the Economy Too. World Economic Forum. https://www.weforum.org/agenda/2018/12/vegetarianism-is-good-for-the-economy-too/

Extra Crispy Staff. (2021). Three-Ingredient Pancakes for When You Literally Can't Even Recipe. MyRecipes. https://www.myrecipes.com/recipe/three-ingredient-pancakes-for-when-you-literally-cant-even

Fact or Fiction: Snack Edition. (2017, July 20). Truly Good Foods. https://www.trulygoodfoods.com/blog/fact-fiction-snack-edition/

Ferdman, Z. (n.d.). Simple Kale Chips Recipe. Tasty. https://tasty.co/recipe/simple-kale-chips

Firoben, J. (n.d.). Cauliflower Hash Browns Recipe by Tasty. Tasty. https://tasty.co/recipe/cauliflower-hash-browns

Fry, S. (2016, June). Overnight Oats & Kefir, Berries, & Toasted Coconut Recipe. MyRecipes. https://www.myrecipes.com/recipe/overnight-oats-kefir-berries-toasted-coconut

Gilson, T. (2017, August 24). Mediterranean Breakfast Burritos. Food Meanderings. https://foodmeanderings.com/healthy-mediterranean-breakfast-burritos/

Grant, L. (2020). Vegetarian Udon Noodle Soup. EatingWell. https://www.eatingwell.com/recipe/279144/vegetarian-udon-noodle-soup/

Haas, S. (2020). Chinese Crispy Noodles with Tofu & Peanut Sauce. EatingWell. https://www.eatingwell.com/recipe/280177/chinese-crispy-noodles-with-tofu-peanut-sauce/

Hackett, J. (2019, November 5). 7 Vegetarian Tips for Healthier Eating. The Spruce Eats. https://www.thespruceeats.com/tips-for-vegetarian-health-3376924

Hardison, K. (2021). Quick Bean and Rice Burritos. Taste of Home. https://www.tasteofhome.com/recipes/quick-bean-and-rice-burritos/

Hatch, C. (n.d.). Garlic Parmesan Roasted Chickpeas Recipe. Tasty.co. https://tasty.co/recipe/garlic-parmesan-roasted-chickpeas

Healthy Food Choices in Schools. (2019, June 12). How School Lunches Can Benefit Your Child. Extension.org. https://healthy-food-choices-in-schools.extension.org/how-school-lunches-can-benefit-your-child/

Heaton, P. (2018, July 9). Flatbread Caprese. Epicurious. https://www.epicurious.com/recipes/food/views/flatbread-caprese-tomato-mozzarella-basil

Hecht, A. (2009, January 7). Vegetarian and Vegan Diets Explained. WebMD; https://www.webmd.com/food-recipes/guide/vegetarian-and-vegan-diet

Horton, B. (2021). Mini Breakfast Pizzas Recipe. MyRecipes. https://www.myrecipes.com/recipe/mini-breakfast-pizzas

Howard, J. (2018, May). Fruit & Cheese Bistro Lunch Box. EatingWell. https://www.eatingwell.com/recipe/264677/fruit-cheese-bistro-lunch-box/

Hulston Corvin, L. (2006, June). Blueberry and Maple-Pecan Granola Parfaits Recipe. MyRecipes. https://www.myrecipes.com/recipe/blueberry-maple-pecan-granola-parfaits

Iannelli, V. (2021, February 13). Are You Raising a Vegetarian Child? Verywell Family. https://www.verywellfamily.com/vegan-and-vegetarian-diets-for-kids-2633962

Iverson, N. (n.d.). General Tso's Cauliflower. Taste of Home. https://www.tasteofhome.com/recipes/general-tso-s-cauliflower/

Izzy. (2016, September 26). Sweet Potato Bites with Black Bean Hummus & Guacamole. She Likes Food. https://www.shelikesfood.com/sweet-potato-bites-black-bean-hummus-guacamole/

Izzy. (2017, February 9). Protein Packed Quinoa Bites with Sweet Potato and Black Beans. She Likes Food. https://www.shelikesfood.com/protein-packed-quinoa-bites-with-sweet-potato-and-black-beans/

Jannine and Jack. (2021, January 21). Tofu Scramble Recipe. Love and Lemons. https://www.loveandlemons.com/tofu-scramble/

Jeanine and Jack. (2016, April 3). Vegan Carrot Waffles Recipe. Love and Lemons. https://www.loveandlemons.com/vegan-carrot-waffles/

Jeanine and Jack. (2019, March 29). Baked Oatmeal Recipe. Love and Lemons. https://www.loveandlemons.com/baked-oatmeal/

Jeannine and Jack. (2019, August 29). Crispy Cauliflower Po' Boy Sandwich Recipe. Love and Lemons. https://www.loveandlemons.com/po-boy-sandwich/

Keep Fruits & Vegetables Fresher Longer. (2021). Heart. https://www.heart.org/en/healthy-living/healthy-eating/add-color/keep-fruits-vegetables-fresher-longer

Kids Health. (2016). Vegetarianism. Kidshealth.org. https://kidshealth.org/en/parents/vegetarianism.html

Kiely, G. (2019). 10 Things You Should Know Before Going Veggie. BBC Good Food. https://www.bbcgoodfood.com/howto/guide/10-things-you-should-know-going-veggie

Killeen, B. (2018, October). Savory Oatmeal with Cheddar, Collards & Eggs. EatingWell. https://www.eatingwell.com/recipe/267654/savory-oatmeal-with-cheddar-collards-eggs/

Kingsley, K. (2019, July 10). It's Easy to Make Your Own Veggie Chips. The Spruce Eats. https://www.thespruceeats.com/homemade-vegetable-chips-102105

Kramer, A. (2019, August 5). Toffee Popcorn Balls. The Spruce Eats. https://www.thespruceeats.com/toffee-popcorn-balls-3371659

Krista. (2017, April 3). Pesto Cream Cheese Strawberry Bruschetta Bites. Joyful Healthy Eats. https://www.joyfulhealthyeats.com/pesto-cream-cheese-strawberry-bruschetta-bites/

Krummel, K. (n.d.). Hearty Italian White Bean Soup. Taste of Home. https://www.tasteofhome.com/recipes/hearty-italian-white-bean-soup/

Kuchera, A. M. (2021). So Your Child Wants To Be a Vegetarian... Kids plus Pediatrics. https://kidspluspgh.com/doctors-notes/so-your-child-wants-to-be-a-vegetarian/

Laliberte, M. (2020, November 16). 13 Healthy Breakfast Mistakes You Might Make This Morning. The Healthy. https://www.thehealthy.com/weight-loss/healthy-breakfast-mistakes/

Largeman-Roth, F. (2015, May). Smoky Egg and Cheese Tostada Recipe. MyRecipes. https://www.myrecipes.com/recipe/smoky-egg-cheese-tostada

Leroy, F., & Cohen, M. (2019, June 29). Why We Shouldn't All Be Vegan. The Conversation. https://theconversation.com/why-we-shouldnt-all-be-vegan-109308

Limas, D. (n.d.). Avocado Quesadillas. Taste of Home. https://www.tasteofhome.com/recipes/avocado-quesadillas/

Link, R. (2018, October 17). The Vegetarian Diet: A Beginner's Guide and Meal Plan. Healthline; https://www.healthline.com/nutrition/vegetarian-diet-plan

Linnell-Olsen, L. (2019). School or Packed Lunch for Their Children? Verywell Family. https://www.verywellfamily.com/school-lunch-vs-packed-lunch-4065361

London, J., & Sassos, S. (2020, January 28). This Is Exactly What to Eat for Breakfast, According to a Nutritionist. Good Housekeeping. https://www.goodhousekeeping.com/health/diet-nutrition/g27684033/what-to-eat-for-breakfast/

Louis, J. (2012, December). Eggs with Chickpeas, Spinach, and Tomato Recipe. MyRecipes. https://www.myrecipes.com/recipe/eggs-chickpeas-spinach-tomato

Marcin, A. (2018, June 28). The Beginner's Guide to Becoming a Vegetarian. Healthline; https://www.healthline.com/health/becoming-vegetarian

Marusinec, L. (2020, October 8). How to Become a Vegetarian As a Kid. WikiHow. https://www.wikihow.com/Become-a-Vegetarian-As-a-Kid

McMordie, K. (2017, February 27). Caramelized Banana Dark Chocolate Oatmeal. Lively Table. https://livelytable.com/caramelized-banana-dark-chocolate-oatmeal/

Melissa, & Doug. (2017, September 30). 4 Vegetarian Playtime Ideas for Kids. Melissa and Doug. https://www.melissaanddoug.com/blogpost/?postId=its-world-vegetarian-day-4-playtime-ideas-for-kids

Mental Floss. (2016, May 20). 7 Reasons Why Breakfast Really Is the Most Important Meal of the Day. Mentalfloss.com. https://www.mentalfloss.com/article/80160/7-reasons-why-breakfast-really-most-important-meal-day

Minimalist Baker. (2012, November 6). Baked Sweet Potato Chips | Minimalist Baker Recipes. Minimalist Baker. https://minimalistbaker.com/baked-sweet-potato-chips/

Mitchell, L. (2016, June 8). When Your Kid Wants to Become a Vegetarian. Healthcare.utah.edu. https://healthcare.utah.edu/healthfeed/postings/2016/06/kids_vegetarian.php

Miyashiro, L. (2016, October 10). Popcorn Cauliflower. Delish. https://www.delish.com/cooking/recipes/a49589/popcorn-cauliflower-recipe/

Miyashiro, L. (2017, October 24). Mac 'N Cheese Waffles. Delish. https://www.delish.com/cooking/recipe-ideas/recipes/a56070/mac-n-cheese-waffles-recipe/

Nelson, E. (2015, July). Roasted Red Pepper Hummus Veggie Wraps Recipe. MyRecipes. https://www.myrecipes.com/recipe/roasted-red-pepper-hummus-veggie-wraps

Nelson, E. (2017, November). Fall Vegetable Curry Recipe. MyRecipes. https://www.myrecipes.com/recipe/fall-vegetable-curry

Oxmoor House. (2021a). Brown Rice Cereal with Vanilla Cream and Berries Recipe. MyRecipes. https://www.myrecipes.com/recipe/instant-pot-brown-rice-cereal-vanilla-cream-berries

Oxmoor House. (2021b). Toasted Almond and Apple Quinoa Recipe. MyRecipes. https://www.myrecipes.com/recipe/instant-pot-toasted-almond-apple-quinoa

Patalsky, K. (n.d.). Apple-White Cheddar Grilled Cheese. Taste of Home. https://www.tasteofhome.com/recipes/apple-white-cheddar-grilled-cheese/

Perry, M. (2018, February 13). 5 Secrets for Cooking Vegetarian Food. EatingWell. https://www.eatingwell.com/article/78014/5-secrets-for-cooking-vegetarian-food/

Petre, A. (2016). 7 Supplements You Need on a Vegan Diet. Healthline. https://www.healthline.com/nutrition/7-supplements-for-vegans

Rachel. (2012, September 2). Apple Cinnamon Fruit Leather. Baked by Rachel |. https://www.bakedbyrachel.com/apple-cinnamon-fruit-leather/

Raina, K. (2019, February 22). 8 Effects of Skipping Breakfast on Your Health. First Cry Parenting. https://parenting.firstcry.com/articles/magazine-is-skipping-breakfast-unhealthy-for-you/

Renda, M., & Fischer, P. (2009). Vegetarian Diets in Children and Adolescents. Pediatrics in Review, 30(1), e1–e8. https://doi.org/10.1542/pir.30-1-e1

Rogers, K. (2019). Calcium Deficiency. In Encyclopædia Britannica. https://www.britannica.com/science/calcium-deficiency

Sabga, T. (2021). Avocado Egg-in-a-Hole Is the Breakfast Frankensandwich You Deserve Recipe. MyRecipes. https://www.myrecipes.com/recipe/avocado-egg-in-a-hole-is-the-breakfast-frankensandwich-you-deserve

Sally. (2016, January 20). Your kids will LOVE these Veggie Nuggets! Real Mom Nutrition. https://www.realmomnutrition.com/veggie-nuggets/

Sandoval, M. (n.d.-a). Asparagus Fries Recipe by Tasty. Tasty. https://tasty.co/recipe/asparagus-fries

Sandoval, M. (n.d.-b). Zucchini Carrot Fritters Recipe by Tasty. Tasty. https://tasty.co/recipe/zucchini-carrot-fritters

Sanford, A. (2016, November 21). Cheesy Apple Bites. Foolproof Living. https://foolproofliving.com/cheesy-apple-bites-2/

School Meals are Essential for Student Health and Learning. (2019, August). FRAC. https://frac.org/wp-content/uploads/School-Meals-are-Essential-Health-and-Learning_FNL.pdf

Southwestern Sweet Potato and Egg Hash Recipe. (2021). MyRecipes. https://www.myrecipes.com/recipe/southwestern-sweet-potato-and-egg-hash

Spritzler, F. (2019, June 19). Is Snacking Good or Bad for You? Healthline; https://www.healthline.com/nutrition/snacking-good-or-bad

Stafford, R. (2019, February 7). A Skeptical Look at Popular Diets: Vegetarian is Healthy if You Tread Carefully. Scope. https://scopeblog.stanford.edu/2019/02/07/a-skeptical-look-at-popular-diets-vegetarian-is-healthy-if-you-tread-carefully/

Steber, C. (2018, February 1). 11 Surprising Ways Your Body Can Change When You Become A Vegetarian. Bustle. https://www.bustle.com/p/11-surprising-ways-your-body-can-change-when-you-become-a-vegetarian-8058927

Taylor Pittman, A. (2016, April). Chocolate Buckwheat Waffles with Juicy Berries Recipe. MyRecipes. https://www.myrecipes.com/recipe/chocolate-buckwheat-waffles-juicy-berries

Taylor, M. (2017, September 19). 7 Signs Your Vegetarian Or Vegan Diet Isn't Working For You. Prevention. https://www.prevention.com/food-nutrition/a20492697/7-signs-your-vegetarian-or-vegan-diet-isn-t-working-for-you/

The Best Vitamins and Supplements for Vegetarians: A Simple Guide. (2021). Takecareof. https://takecareof.com/articles/what-vitamins-should-vegetarians-take

The Spruce. (2019, July 4). Healthy Banana Split On A Stick. The Spruce Eats. https://www.thespruceeats.com/banana-splits-on-a-stick-4133895

Treon, R. (2020, January 29). The Meat-Eating Family's Guide to Eating Less Meat. Allrecipes. https://www.allrecipes.com/article/how-to-feed-family-vegetarian/

Turnbull, C. (n.d.). Colorful Quinoa Salad. Taste of Home. https://www.tasteofhome.com/recipes/colorful-quinoa-salad/

Vegan Richa. (2014, June 13). Vegan Chocolate Chip Cookie Dough Bars. No Bake Gluten Free. Vegan Richa. https://www.veganricha.com/chocolate-chip-cookie-dough-bars-no/

Vegetarian Diets for Children and Teenagers. (2021). Raising Children Network. https://raisingchildren.net.au/school-age/nutrition-fitness/healthy-eating-habits/vegetarian-diets-teenagers

Vegetarian Diets for Children and Teens. (2021). Caring for Kids. https://www.caringforkids.cps.ca/handouts/healthy-living/vegetarian_diets_for_children_and_teens

Vegetarian Times Editors. (2007, June 16). 16 Reasons You Should Go Veg. Vegetarian Times. https://www.vegetariantimes.com/health-nutrition/plant-based-diet/why-go-veg-learn-about-becoming-a-vegetarian/

Vegetarianism and Religion. (2019). Drexel.edu. http://www.pages.drexel.edu/~soa29/Religious%20Issues.htm

Vilsack, T. (2013, May 3). Why Healthy School Meals Matter. Health.com; https://www.health.com/family/why-healthy-school-meals-matter

Von Alt, S. (2017, August 7). What to Do If Your Kid Decides to Go Vegetarian. ChooseVeg. https://chooseveg.com/blog/heres-what-to-do-if-your-kid-decides-to-go/

Wall, P. (2018, December 10). I Cooked My Family Vegetarian Dinners for 30 Days and Here's What Happened. EatingWell. https://www.eatingwell.com/article/291376/i-cooked-my-family-vegetarian-dinners-for-30-days-and-heres-what-happened/

Ward, L. (2015, November 12). No Beef Allowed: Inside the Schools That Have Banned Meat. The Guardian. https://www.theguardian.com/teacher-network/2015/nov/12/no-beef-allowed-inside-schools-banned-meat

Weisenberger, J. (2015, June 29). What Science Says about Snacking. Food & Nutrition Magazine. https://foodandnutrition.org/july-august-2015/science-says-snacking/

White, R. R., & Hall, M. B. (2017). Nutritional and Greenhouse Gas Impacts of Removing Animals From US Agriculture. Proceedings of the National Academy of Sciences, 114(48), E10301–E10308. https://doi.org/10.1073/pnas.1707322114

Wise, D. (2021). Breakfast Bowl with Tomato, Avocado, and Egg Recipe. MyRecipes. https://www.myrecipes.com/recipe/breakfast-bowl-tomato-avocado-egg

Yeager, D. (2021). Public School Vegetarian Menu Still a Hit After Two Years. Todays Dietitian. https://www.todaysdietitian.com/enewsletter/enews_0715_01.shtml

Zied, E. (2013, May 8). Should Kids Eat a Vegetarian School Lunch? Parents. https://www.parents.com/recipes/scoop-on-food/should-kids-eat-a-vegetarian-school-lunch/

IMAGE REFERENCES

Figure 1: Intro. From Unsplash, by Brooke Lark, 2017. https://unsplash.com/photos/jUPOXXRNdcA

Figure 2: Vegetarian Diet. From Unsplash, by Sharon Pittaway, 2018. https://unsplash.com/photos/KUZnfk-2DSQ

Figure 3: Supplements. From Unsplash, by Michele Blackwell, 2019. https://unsplash.com/photos/przZDqzZKpk

Figure 4: Why Vegetarian. From Unsplash, by Libby Penner, 2019. https://unsplash.com/photos/kdN1eyuuqcE

Figure 5: Things to Consider. From Unsplash, by Melissa Walker Horn, 2019. https://unsplash.com/photos/A_Xr_1HWFXo

Figure 6: Cooking With Kids. From Unsplash, by Annie Spratt, 2020. https://unsplash.com/photos/UyEmagArOLY

Figure 7: Danger Signs. From Unsplash, by Vitolda Klein, 2021. https://unsplash.com/photos/1TfFiHeZZ3Q

Figure 8: Healthy Food. From Unsplash, by Anna Pelzer, 2017. https://unsplash.com/photos/IGfIGP5ONV0

Figure 9: Breakfast Casserole. From Unsplash, by Jonathan Pielmayer, 2018. https://unsplash.com/photos/RKJElwIyCQw

Figure 10: Granola Parfait. From Unsplash, by Alisha Hieb, 2017. https://unsplash.com/photos/LzrMzmVWhJw

Figure 11: Pancakes. From Unsplash, by Luke Pennystan, 2018. https://unsplash.com/photos/09FcOqmi8R0

Figure 12: Snacking. From Unsplash, by Kelly Sikkema, 2017. https://unsplash.com/photos/PMxoh8zJNb0

Figure 13: Nachos. From Unsplash, by Evan Reimer, 2019. https://unsplash.com/photos/EVMuKNg0FOE

Figure 14: Kale Chips. From Unsplash, by Charles Deluvio, 2018. https://unsplash.com/photos/la6DtkODelg

Figure 15: Soft Pretzel. From Unsplash, by Markus Spiske, 2019. https://unsplash.com/photos/39cEDqW5_SY

Figure 16: Lunchbox. From Unsplash, by Ella Olsson, 2018. https://unsplash.com/photos/sosOqjx31Go

Figure 17: Flatbread Pizza. From Unsplash, by Laure Noverraz, 2021. https://unsplash.com/photos/gujFRz2nHVY

Figure 18: Veggie Lasagna. From Unsplash, by Angèle Kamp, 2019. https://unsplash.com/photos/WpnGOZ3C5uU

Figure 19: Veggie Wraps. From Unsplash, by Ella Olsson, 2018. https://unsplash.com/photos/6UxD0NzDywI

Figure 20: Vegetarian Family. From Unsplash, by Lino Ogenio, 2021. https://unsplash.com/photos/45gpNuPhhOs